Facing Feelings
in Faith Communities

Facing Feelings
in Faith Communities

William M. Kondrath

 ALBAN

Herndon, Virginia
www.alban.org

The Alban Institute
131 Elden St., Suite 202
Herndon, VA 20170

"Grief" by Malika Lueen Ndlovu, from *The Truth is Both Spirit and Flesh,* copyright © 2008 by Malika Lueen Ndlovu. Reprinted by permission of the author.

"letting go in autumn," copyright © 2011 by Toni Stuart. Preprinted by permission of Toni Stuart.

"I Give You Back." Copyright © 1983 Joy Harjo, from SHE HAD SOME HORSES by Joy Harjo. Used by permission of W. W. Norton & Company, Inc.

"Fern Hill," by Dylan Thomas, from THE POEMS OF DYLAN THOMAS, copyright ©1945 by The Trustees for the Copyrights of Dylan Thomas. Reprinted by permission of New Directions Publishing Corp.

"Do Not Go Gentle into That Good Night," by Dylan Thomas, from THE POEMS OF DYLAN THOMAS, copyright ©1952 by Dylan Thomas. Reprinted by permission of New Directions Publishing Corp.

Unless otherwise noted, all Scripture quotations are from the New Revised Standard Version of the Bible, copyright © 1989, Division of Christian Education of the National Council of the Churches of Christ in the United States of America, and are used by permission.

The cover design is an abstract composition created by overlapping the illustrations that open chapters in *Facing Feelings.* Each illustration represents a feeling, and together they express the complex and occasionally chaotic challenge of responding to the diverse emotions found within a congregation.
Cover design by Daniel Belen, DBL Design Group.
Illustrations: "Fear," "Anger," "Sadness," "Peace," "Power," "Joy," "Substitution," and "Shame" copyright © 2012 by Rachel Robb Kondrath. Printed by permission. www.RachelRobbKondrath.com

Library of Congress Cataloging-in-Publication Data
    Kondrath, William M.
     Facing feelings in faith communities / William M. Kondrath.
       pages cm
     Includes bibliographical references and index.
     ISBN 978-1-56699-434-7 (alk. paper)
     1. Emotions--Religious aspects--Christianity. I. Title.
     BV4597.3.K66 2013
     248.4--dc23
                       2013001235

13   14   15   16   17   V P   5   4   3   2   1

For Chris, Susannah, and Rachel
who continue to grace-fully face all manner of feelings with me.

Contents

Foreword

If you hold this book, then you share some interest in learning about the power of feelings in faith communities. You should be warned that it might have just as easily been titled, *A Guide to Liberation for Privileged People*. Because that is precisely what Bill Kondrath has created.

Racism, sexism, heterosexism, and classism deliver incalculable privilege to people who are not the targets of oppression. But they also cost them—cost us—dearly. To prove you are worthy of the power you have been granted, you have to play by the rules. You must bottle up your feelings and show the world a calm, cool, and trustworthy exterior, and you must distance yourself from culture groups that get painted as hot, emotional, and un-balanced. In my experience as both insider (Harvard graduate, Episcopal priest, member of a bishop's senior staff) and margin dweller (black, single woman from the working-class South, still a "young adult" in the eyes of the church), I have learned that the surest way to assimilate and rise to power is by cutting the cord to your feeling self.

To see this narrative play out on a national stage, one need only witness America's first black president, Barack Obama, and his legendary, preternatural "cool." My favorite sketch comedy show, *Key & Peele*, stars two mixed-race comedians from Chicago who have a special vantage for viewing Obama's quandary. In one recurring skit, Jordan Peele plays President Obama in the Oval Office, offering reasoned commentary on the issues of the day. His every word is considered, every emotion carefully calibrated. By his side is Luther, "The Anger Translator." Luther jumps up and down, waves his hands, kicks and curses, and generally expresses the anger, sadness, and frustration that a president can never show, especially if he is a black man. Power equals cool. Obama has it. Luther cannot.

Granted, we do not need a president who shoots off in anger. A CEO who is swamped by fear cannot hope to be effective. And clergy who are utterly wound up in their own emotional turmoil have far less heart space to feel compassion for others. But those are the extremes. Contrary to the dominant European-American narrative, feelings are not automatically enemies to power or effective leadership. They are an essential part of how we know, how we act, how we connect and how we move compassionately in the world. There is no way to be a leader, and certainly not a Christian leader, without being tuned in to the powerful wisdom that only comes from our feelings.

In the pages that follow, Bill Kondrath calculates the steep cost of being cut off from our feelings and then outlines the steps toward gaining "affective competence." I trust him in this work as I trust no one else, for I have seen him practice it for more than a decade, first as my professor and mentor at Episcopal Divinity School, then as a trusted colleague in ministry in the Boston area, and finally as a consultant for The Crossing, the emergent congregation I founded with a community of young adults in Boston. Bill is brave enough to mine his own story and to model vulnerability even as he invites us into it. At the very same time, he draws on cutting edge scholarship and gathers pearls from his extensive personal experience as a priest, professor, counselor, and consultant. The combination of resources and wisdom Bill has assembled here is powerful, compelling, practical, and essential for today's Christian leaders.

The church needs this book, and perhaps never more so than at this critical moment in Christian history. We are swirling in the midst of an era of unprecedented change. Demographic patterns, technological developments, and theological alignments are shifting faster than anyone can keep up with. While those quakes inevitably hit the margins first, they have now reverberated into the mainline. A new church is groaning into existence, and no denomination or tradition will emerge unaffected. If people are going to embrace and cooperate with this movement of the Spirit, rather than erect blockades and resist change, we need to learn to work with unresolved, unnamed, unacknowledged feelings.

As Bill argues, preparing for transformation requires acquiring a feeling language. Specifically, we need practice touching and then expressing our grief at the loss of identity. Congregations need to speak of the overwhelming fear that the church as we have known it may disappear. We need room for the roiling anger that anyone would reject the church and traditions we have loved so deeply. Just as importantly, we need to get in touch with our joy at feeling intimacy with God. We need a language to express the peace we feel when we truly connect to each other and to our deepest, truest selves. And we desperately need permission to own the power we feel when we create new possibilities hand in hand with God.

When I imagine the church I want to be part of, the community I long to help create, I see a church that is vulnerable, honest, wise, loving, and capable of engaging the full range of human experience and emotion. It is unafraid, including as it faces its own fears. It is angry in the face of oppression and injustice. It is joyful in the presence of God. I picture something like Howard Thurman's kingdom vision of a "friendly world of friendly folk beneath a friendly sky." Bill Kondrath has created a resource that moves people, congregations, and institutions closer to that reality. For the blessing of this book and the suite of accompanying resources, and for the gift of Bill's dedication to liberation for all people, I am deeply grateful.

The Reverend Canon Stephanie Spellers
Canon for Missional Vitality in the Episcopal
Diocese of Long Island
Author, Radical Welcome: Embracing God, The Other
and the Spirit of Transformation

Acknowledgments

This book has two sets of parents: students in classes I have taught on campus and online through Episcopal Divinity School, and participants in workshops, board retreats, and clergy days I have led in Florida, Connecticut, New Hampshire, Massachusetts, Colorado, Illinois, and Michigan, at the Sorrento Center in British Columbia, and in Edmonton, Alberta. With each group, I learned as much as I taught. I nuanced my thinking as I became more in touch with what I was feeling in response to new questions, objections, and suggestions.

My own contributions are greatly enhanced by the illustrations of my daughter, Rachel Robb Kondrath. A production designer by trade, Rachel is deeply familiar with the theory of feelings I have presented here, because she herself is involved in antiracism training and multicultural consulting, which use some of this theory. I am grateful for both her evocative art and the patience with which she engaged in the tricky dynamics and affective intricacies that are involved in a father-daughter working partnership.

Beth Gaede believed in me and in this book when it was an outline I drafted on a ride to New Hampshire for a getaway weekend. Beth bought into the idea of supplementing the book with art, and sold that idea to Richard Bass and others at Alban. She also clarified my at times fuzzy thinking and awkward expressions and introduced me to companions who supported and stretched my affective journey. I did not imagine that this second writing-editing adventure would be even better than the first. It was.

Andrea Lee helped me with the details of permissions for the works from which I have borrowed. Her attention to detail in that research and in copyediting meant that I had the stamina to stay with this project long after the more enjoyable creative process was mostly wrapped up.

Colleagues at VISIONS, Inc., and at Episcopal Divinity School have provided much of the conceptual grounding and daily practice that undergird this book, and I continue to be grateful to them.

Nicole le Roux, Lisa Hess, Debbie Little, Shenandoah Gale, Katherine Stiles, Laura Ahrens, Brian Dench, Jim Gorman, and Pat Dunn offered encouragement, support, and concrete suggestions during the early stages of formation and writing. Peter Soltz and I have shared coffee and affective conversations after early mornings at the gym for more years than either of us will ever admit.

My life partner, Chris Robb, suggested poems and tracked them down in her library. She offered support when I was discouraged. She reminded me why this project was important. Perhaps most important, for more than three decades she has helped me face my feelings. She has faced them with me, and she has often been the one to point out my patterns of affective substitution when I was too afraid or sad to see them. On more than one occasion she has reminded me, "I have never felt worse after crying." It has been a joy to learn more deeply about my emotional life with such a perceiving and empathetic partner.

Introduction

I am an educated white clergyman of European descent (half Hungarian with some Transylvanian and Irish thrown in). When I grew up, we didn't talk at all about feelings in our family, and the patterns of emotional expression were pretty set. For example, my dad was the only one allowed to express anger, even though we all felt angry at times. I remember feeling angry and occasionally expressing my anger and being told in no uncertain terms that it was not okay to be angry. So when I couldn't be angry, I expressed sadness instead. It didn't work! Instead of getting some recognition for what I perceived to be a wrong done to me or an injustice I had observed, I was asked, "What are you sad about?" I had no answer. I knew I wasn't sad, and I also knew I couldn't say I was angry.

To complicate things as I grew older, I was getting messages from other boys, from TV, and from relatives that "big boys don't cry." Pretty soon I found it easier not to express any emotions, except maybe to be mildly content or peaceful—whether I really felt that way or not.

Only much later did I realize I wasn't alone. As I have conducted classes, retreats, and workshops about the role of emotions in our individual and congregational lives, many people have reported families of origin similar to mine. The types of emotions that were expressly forbidden, or passively allowed, may have varied. The common thread was that most people reported they were patterned or socialized into believing that only some emotions were okay to have or to express. The messages they received about permissible and forbidden emotional expressions were sometimes overt and sometimes transmitted only by inference. With reflection, people could name the emotional expressions that were rewarded and those that were ignored, discouraged, or punished. With guidance and encouragement they could also uncover and bring to consciousness the feelings they learned to substitute for those that they were told were unacceptable. And like me, people realized that the emotions they had learned to substitute, for survival purposes, didn't really get them what they needed or wanted. They bought time or brought temporary peace, but always at the cost of being authentic and expressing what felt real and true.

I believe faith communities are filled with lots of men like me and with women who were trained or conditioned, in somewhat different ways, to express only certain feelings permitted to them in *their* families. I also believe that these patterns of permission, denial, and substitution are a matter of early familial and social conditioning. The substitutions were taught or caught, *and* they can be unlearned. As adults we can unlearn these patterned responses and choose to reconnect to our feelings in ways that are more congruent with the realities we experience. When we feel a violation of our boundaries or a major thwarting of our expectations, we can express anger about the situation, rather than substitute sadness, if that is the pattern we learned as children. That is, we can reprogram our emotional software!

Simply put, we have emotions because we need them. They give us messages about what is happening within us and around us—messages that help us navigate life and make important decisions. God created us as affectively competent beings. I believe the original emotional software that came with our neurological wiring was meant to help us understand our world and to give appropriate signals to people around us about what we are experiencing so that they can choose how to respond. Unfortunately, for many of us, our emotional software was infected early on with viruses that distorted the way we respond to natural stimuli.

Facing Feelings in Faith Communities (in both its print version and its electronic format) is an attempt to help individuals restore our emotional systems to their original state, or at least to invite us to imagine how we would live differently if our emotional expressions were more nearly congruent with the situations and events we encounter—without the interference of parental prohibitions and rewards that have narrowly limited our emotional expressions. *Congregational Resources for Facing Feelings* is a companion collection in which I offer examples of how our life in community would be enriched if we and those around us were as emotionally competent as we are intellectually capable and behaviorally skilled.

The book you are reading is an invitation to explore your emotional life by looking at six primary feelings or groups of feelings: fear, anger, sadness, peace, power (agency, not dominance), and joy. The exploration of these feelings will be poetic and meditative as well as discursive. My hope is to evoke the experience of these affective states and to describe them and the messages they offer to help us interpret and respond to our world. I invite you to begin your exploration by sitting with a drawing. For some of us, visual stimuli are more provocative than words. Spend time with the image provided in the chapter or turn to images of your own. Notice what comes up for you immediately and as you spend time with the image. Allow yourself to notice *where* you feel fear or anger or joy in your body. As you explore these feelings, I encourage you to read some poetry and scripture and to immerse yourself in your own experience and personal history. In much the same way that you have explored your cognitive or intellectual capacities, allow yourself to know the emotional dimensions of who you are and how God created you. Allow yourself to exercise your emotional muscles in ways similar to how you have explored your physical muscles in learning a new sport, such as playing tennis, or exercising dexterity through knitting or needlepoint.

I will also briefly mention shame and guilt. They are more complicated feelings and distinct from the primary feelings that are the focus of this book. They do, however, play a major role in many lives, so I will set them in context and suggest resources for further exploration.

Each chapter's consideration of the six primary feeling families begins with what the feeling is like for individuals, how we experience the feeling individually, and what message the feeling carries that will help us understand and interpret our current circumstances and what we may need. Then I will ask what connection the feeling under consideration is inviting us to make. How does anger or fear or sadness position us in relationship to others? How does being joyful or peaceful or powerful affect those around us? I will also explore the role gender plays in how we are socialized to notice and express these various feelings. Are men and women given different latitude in expressing anger or sadness? What role does gender play in the ways we are allowed to feel powerful? I will also suggest what a congregation that primarily exhibits one of these feeling families might look like. As you read you will be invited to notice the systemic way particular congregations or agencies absorb and display feelings. Most of us have probably experienced *joyful* congregations or *sad* faith communities or community groups that are *afraid* they are dying or won't be funded.

Having delved into the various feeling families and encouraged you to reflect on how each major feeling resonates within you, I will invite you to explore the theory of *substitution of feelings*. Simply put, this theory suggests that most of us, at a very early age, learned to substitute an *acceptable* feeling for one that was not allowed or valued in our family of origin. Because the feeling congruent with our experience was banned or undervalued, we *put on* or enacted a feeling deemed okay within our family system, even if we knew it didn't really fit what we were experiencing. I will also explore the cost of such substitution. Though we may have felt at the time that we had little choice in the substitution, we probably paid a price for not expressing a more authentic feeling—for not showing up as fully as we may have wished. At the time, it may have been our only choice. The significant, on-going cost for us is the unreflective, learned pattern and its lack of usefulness as we grow older.

One assumption I, along with a number of theorists, make is that babies naturally express feelings *congruent* with the stimulus that evokes them. Generally, young infants are startled or frightened when they hear a loud noise. They are angry when their expectation to be fed or have a diaper changed is not met. They are sad when left alone too long or when a comforting parent puts them down. And their parents are generally pretty good at distinguishing the difference between the expressions of these emotions. Angry cries sound different from frightened cries or sad cries. Infants also express other feelings congruently. They are peaceful after nursing or while being cuddled. They are joyful when playing with a mobile. And as they get older, they have a sense of power or agency when they learn the meaning of words or take their first steps. Observing this natural congruency is important, because it allows us to see how our emotional software is meant to function when substitution has not tinkered with the stimulus → response dynamic.

As you read *Facing Feelings in Faith Communities*, you will be invited to experience your own natural emotions, I hope with little interference from substitutions. For some people, connecting to and identifying emotions is relatively easy. For others, one or two emotions feel comfortable or easily recognizable; others are hard to connect to or feel foreign. There are even people who say, "I don't really feel many emotions" or "I don't do feelings." If you identify with the latter folks, I invite you to explore how much your lack of access to your feelings is conditioned by your family of origin, your ethnicity or culture, or all three—and also to ask *how* that limited emotional access served you as you were growing up. But mostly, I encourage each reader to attempt to access the emotional processes that came with your cognitive and kinesthetic package of functions at birth, or perhaps even in the womb.

The companion to this book, *Congregational Resources for Facing Feelings,* is an electronic collection of practical applications or case studies that look at several congregational situations in which exercising greater emotional competence will improve our understanding of what is happening and the effectiveness of our actions and those of others. These applications can be purchased as a collection or as individual downloads. My thesis in the applications is that because we are underutilizing our emotional capacities, or misusing them, we are missing out on the opportunity to live and work as our best selves, fully utilizing all the capacities that God gave us.

When I am consulting, I frequently speak about open systems. Or I hear clients talk about the desire for more transparent leadership. Most often the discussion turns to communicating ideas or goals. Sometimes the conversation is about underlying, hidden assumptions and making them clear to all parties. I label all this *cognitive transparency.* In these conversations, rarely do people include the clear and open communication of feelings. And yet my experience has been that when leaders hide their feelings from other staff members, coworkers, volunteers, and parishioners or clients, the waters get much murkier than when assumptions, goals, and rationales are hidden or unexplained. And the confusion or obstruction happens more rapidly when feelings are hidden or opaque than when cognitive assumptions are hidden or ideas are unclear. Obviously, this is not an either-or situation. However, it is my belief that the technology most groups employ in exposing assumptions, goals, and leadership theory and practice is much more developed and accessible than the technology for articulating feelings and examining how they affect our relationships and our work. This book and the accompanying applications are an attempt to help individuals and groups move toward greater *affective transparency.*

Since this is a book about feelings, I will also quickly add that many people are more scared or afraid of exploring the impact of feelings than they are about exploring ideas and beliefs. This should not surprise anyone, since most leaders and followers are well schooled in cognitive and behavioral skills. Few are formally educated in affective theory or skills. I often ask students in the leadership classes I teach where a person goes to become affectively competent or where they learned to recognize and understand their own feelings. As graduate students, they are well educated cognitively, and many have acquired significant behavior skills, such as public speaking, preaching, and functioning liturgically, not to mention skills such as playing golf or tennis. But few have attended a university, a class, or even a single workshop to learn about their own feelings or to be better able to attend to, read, and respond to the feelings of others.

How to Use This Book and Its Companion Applications

There is no right way to become affectively competent. Some readers will primarily be interested in one or two feelings and how they operate personally or institutionally. Others will want to delve immediately into the practical applications of how being more affectively competent will increase membership or enhance the educational programs for children or adults. Others will look for advice for dealing with problematic congregational board meetings where anger or fear is a constant underlying reality. Whatever your reasons for coming to the work of affective competence, I invite you to explore your responses to this material with other people. How our emotions affect everything we see and do is seldom talked about in any depth. *Facing Feelings in Faith Communities* will help you to initiate a cultural change in your faith community and in your home. You can't do that alone. And as soon as you begin to talk more openly about what you are experiencing emotionally and encourage others to join you, *you have begun the cultural shift.*

Though you may be tempted to skip over the artwork, poetry, quotations, and scripture that start each chapter of this book, I encourage you to dwell there for a while. Often in art and poetry we are able to recapture our innate emotional processes. For this reason, each feeling chapter will begin with an *invitation to experience* the feeling under consideration. We are so used to reading books for intellectual content or pointers on how to behave differently that I urge you to immerse yourself in each feeling. Think of it, if you will, as being baptized into the various emotional states that God has given you for your well-being and salvation. If need be, consider having a *baptismal sponsor* for each feeling or for your emotional life as a whole—some individual, or group of people, who you believe exemplifies a healthy affective life. You might actually speak with your sponsor about your journey, or perhaps she or he is a departed *ancestor* or *ancient one*, or someone who accompanies you in spirit.

If the artwork and the selections you read are not evocative enough for you, recall and explore your own favorite quotations or look through a book of photographs or paintings and allow yourself to feel what you see. Think of your favorite hymns, classical music, operas, or contemporary songs—music for different seasons and different moods. Ask yourself what movie, painting, or music illustrates or orchestrates each feeling family for you.

Whether you read the text privately or with a group, ponder the reflection questions. Give yourself permission to breathe in the feelings as they are evoked in each chapter. The greatest benefit from this book will come when you can experience in your body what the text suggests and when you can imagine different scenarios and outcomes for routine events and practices.

Place yourself in a provocative space to read this text: a museum, an art gallery, an outdoor mall, a scenic beach. My daughter Rachel, who drew the images included in this book, is a visual artist. Her room is filled with mobiles pinned to the ceiling—paper origami doves, umbrellas, spinning strips of plastic, dancing cloth figurines. One wall is nearly covered with a gigantic poster of *Sgt. Pepper's Lonely Hearts Club Band,* and on the crowded book shelf below it is a picture of her at a candlelight vigil at the state house, protesting the death penalty. Visiting her room pulls me out of my normal frame of reference and invites me to a place of wonder and awe.

My hope is that this book will be a creative environment for you to journey into your own soul territory—to experience and embody feelings in a way that you can befriend them as never before. For some of us, this type of exploration comes easy. It is how we go through life. The difficulty is that the institutions of which we are a part don't encourage this journey. Some of us have more difficulty finding and claiming our affective selves. We value our cognitive selves and place great merit on what we and others do or accomplish. Perhaps we were even instructed not to pay attention to our emotions because they were considered ephemeral or deceptive. This book does not suggest that you need to choose one way of being over another. There are plenty of books on how to think clearly and act justly. My invitation is simply to explore the possibility of giving due diligence to the affective dimension of who we are. It has changed how I see the world and the way I participate in all the relationships that matter the most to me.

The book *Facing Feelings in Faith Communities* will stand alone if you are interested in learning more deeply about how feelings operate in your life and how early patterns of substituting a more socially acceptable feeling for the more natural or congruent feeling leads to problems. For example, people may easily misinterpret what you are really feeling, and you are less likely to get what you need or want. While this book contains many examples that elaborate and illustrate the theory of affective competence, most readers will want to investigate particular applications of the theory in their chosen ministry area.

If your learning style begins with practical questions or starts with concrete problem solving, I invite you to purchase the collection of applications or those specific downloads that you are most interested in. Read those applications in conjunction with the theory of feelings contained in this book. The collection of applications has a brief introduction that refers to the book you are reading, and each individual application contains the "Feelings as Messengers Chart" (see appendix A), which presents the messages that accompany the six basic feelings. Thus, should you choose to share a particular application with youth ministers or stewardship leaders, they will have a guide for better understanding both their feelings and the attendant messages that can help guide the decisions they make.

How Terms Are Used

One of the more difficult aspects of writing about feelings is the set of terms we use for a very complex set of physical and neural processes we call emotions and the various expressions or representations of them—our feelings. While I have aimed for consistency of usage, I have found that different contexts call for different figures of speech. I trust the reader to understand that whether I am using *fear* or *afraid* or *scared*, I am talking about the same feeling family. And while it is important to make some distinctions between *fear* and *anxiety* or between being *mad, angry, irritated,* or *slightly irked,* in each case we are talking about a particular feeling family that carries a similar message. And while distinguishing between the nuances *within* the family has the merit of avoiding some confusion, the greater problem occurs when an unconscious substitution of one feeling family occurs for a dif-

ferent feeling family. Such substitutions confuse those around us
and we rarely get what we want or need as a result.

Bearing in mind that feelings can be expressed as nouns or
as adjectives describing how I feel, I have referred to the feeling
families in both ways: fear (scared), anger (mad), sadness (sad),
peace (peaceful), power or agency (powerful), and joy (joyful).

Feelings are not right or wrong. And I am aware that I do
not always express the feeling most apropos to the situation I
am experiencing—that is, I sometimes *substitute* expressing a
feeling I was permitted to show as a child for a feeling I was not
permitted to show. I use the term *congruence* to indicate that the
feeling being expressed is apropos to the situation (or stimulus)
as I experience it. It may be that two people in a similar situation
have different experiences. My daughter was excited or joyful
whenever she caught a garden snake. My wife was apprehensive,
perhaps afraid. Two women hiking on a narrow trail on the edge
of a steep ravine may experience different feelings: one exhilaration
(joy), one trepidation (fear). Each might be congruent with the
stimulus she experiences. Substitution would occur if either one
was expressing a feeling because of a learned habit that did not
let her express joy, in the first case, or fear, in the second case. I
will offer further explanation and more examples in the chapter
on substitution and projection.

I am interested in how people who identify as men and people
who identify as women might experience feelings differently. This
topic has become increasing complex as scientists and those who
advocate civil rights have begun to distinguish between *biological
sex* (objectively measurable organs, hormones, and chromosomes),
gender identity (how you think about yourself in your head, based
on the chemistry that composes you and how you interpret that),
and *gender expression* (how you demonstrate your gender—based
on traditional gender roles—through the ways you act, dress,
behave, and interact).[1] A biological scientist might want to measure different physical responses (heart rate, body temperature,
rate of respiration, and so forth) and correlate it to people with
biological differences along the spectrum of female-intersex-male.
My interest is more in asking whether how we were socialized

to understand ourselves as women and men (gender identity) conditioned us to view expressing certain feelings as more or less acceptable or prohibited. And further, are there some common substitution patterns that have a high correlation with women and with men? It is *not* my intention to generalize to all women or all men. Rather, I wish to make discussable how men and women *may* experience the same feeling differently, *may* have more or less societal permission or inhibition about expressing various feelings, and *may* talk in different ways about their feelings. Thus when I talk about fear and gender, or anger and gender, I invite you to consider how your experience is similar to the experience of those who share the same gender identity and perhaps different from those who share another gender identity. Because I am focusing on how we have been, and continue to be, socialized in regard to our gender identity, I suspect that there are differences in experience based on generational differences. The purpose is to make all these differences discussable in the service of becoming more affectively competent.

We are living in an age when significant research is being done on emotions and their role in decision making,[2] and on emotions and their role in maintaining, healing, and deepening relationships.[3] Much of this research is taking place in the area of neurology and is beyond the scope of this book. The research scientists and practitioners writing in these areas are attempting to explain in detail how our emotional systems work at the chemical and neurological level. My aim is more modest. I hope to articulate rather simple messages delivered by these emotional systems that give us clues to what we need and want. Thus I will tend to use the terms *emotions* and *feelings* fairly interchangeably, much as they are used in common speech. However, in the interest of acknowledging current research, let me say that *feelings* are what arise as the brain interprets emotions, which are the body's complex physical reactions to external stimuli. For example, the feeling of being afraid arises in our brain when it senses and interprets a set of physical changes including our heart racing, our mouths becoming dry, our skin turning pale, and our muscles contracting. The emotional (physical, bodily) reactions occur automatically and unconsciously.[4] The feeling, fear, occurs when the brain becomes aware of the physical changes and compares them to similar neural maps in the brain's memory. To complicate things a little further, some chemical changes (and thus feelings) can arise simply from changes in the brain mapping center. For example, when we feel sympathy for an injured person, we recreate their pain within our brain, not in response to a current physical stimulus. Also, under extreme stress or fear, the brain appears to be able to turn off the stimulus connection and act as though it were experiencing no pain.[5]

I offer this simple schema for how emotions and feelings work (I hope without doing injustice to the groundbreaking work being done on the level of neurology and biochemistry):

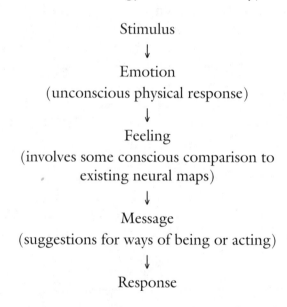

Stimulus
↓
Emotion
(unconscious physical response)
↓
Feeling
(involves some conscious comparison to existing neural maps)
↓
Message
(suggestions for ways of being or acting)
↓
Response

In the six feeling chapters that follow, I will offer a simplified version of this schema for each feeling: stimulus → feeling → message → need or response. This simplified version is easy to remember and offers a way to use our feelings (once we recognize them and check to see that they are congruent and not substitutes) to make better decisions individually and in community.

The messages or suggestions that flow from a particular feeling will be discussed in the chapter about that feeling.

In summary, my hope is to offer readers better access to our God-given emotion and feeling software. This software, through often subtle or dismissed changes in our body, allows us to apprehend messages that assist us in regulating life and relationships. Developing the capacity to notice and read our feelings increases the chances that we will know what we need or want. As we express our feelings more clearly, other people are more likely to respond in ways that are helpful to us, thus enhancing our relationships and the work we might engage together.

1

Three Dimensions of Learning and Change

As we look at the role of feelings in faith communities, it is important to situate the affective dimension alongside the cognitive and behavioral dimension of learning and transformation. Individuals grow and change and interact with other people and our environment in three interrelated dimensions. We contemplate, test out, and acquire new ideas (cognitive learning). We explore new feelings; we notice bodily sensations that carry messages about what we may need (affective learning). And we try out new ways of moving and acting (behavioral learning). The figure below shows one way to imagine those three dimensions of learning.

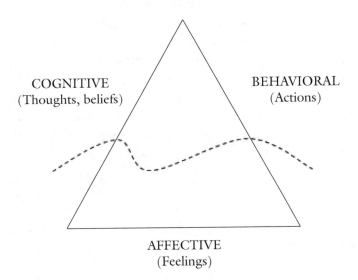

Figure 1. Three Dimensions of Learning and Change
The wavy line represents the fact that the affective dimension of change is like an iceberg and often lies below the surface.

Individuals take in information from all three dimensions. For some people, cognition is the primary way of learning. They are conceptual learners. They read the directions about how to assemble something before they even open the packages that contain the parts. I recently bought a new snowblower and before I unpacked the box, I took out the instruction booklet and read all the way through it. I had my old snowblower for more than twelve years and made most of the repairs on it myself, including fashioning a new wheel for the tread drive. But in this case, I chose to use my cognitive way of learning before assembling and trying out the new machine.

Other people are behavioral learners. They learn by doing. These folks don't bother with the "Read Me" computer files or the bright-colored package inserts that say "Read all the instructions carefully before beginning assembly." They immediately install new software and begin to play with it to see how it works. These are the people who go to the driving range and hit buckets of balls to learn or improve a new golf stroke. They are not likely to watch a golf instructional video or read a book by a golf pro.

Others learn primarily through their emotions. Such people sometimes talk about having a feel for something or knowing it intuitively. Such a person might have a mental list of all the characteristics he or she wants in a new home (large yard, proximity to public transportation, three bedrooms, patio or deck, double garage, ground level entrance, and so forth) and after having been shown several homes that meet these qualifications, hasn't seen the right house. The frustrated realtor shows the potential buyer another home that meets far fewer of the alleged criteria, and the person says, "This is the one. It feels just right." And it turns out the buyer is still delighted with the purchase years later. The buyer *knew* it was right affectively.

No one way of learning is right. Each of us likely has a default manner of learning—at least for most circumstances. Some of us avoid one manner of learning because we have little experience with it or we have deemed it inferior. Some of us are skilled at more than one method of learning, depending on the circumstances. These individual differences are important to keep in mind when working with other people, whether in a family, on a board or committee, or as a member of a staff. Coming at a complicated problem or a difficult community transition using all three methods of analysis and learning—cognitive, affective, and behavioral—has advantages. The cognitive approach allows an individual or group to gather data, examine biases, weigh the pros and cons of a particular approach, and present rationales for a particular decision. The behavioral approach values the idea that certain changes can be evaluated only by experimenting or trying on practices and behaviors. For example, introducing new music on a trial basis allows an evaluation of the congregation's ability to sing new rhythms or styles. Paying attention to feelings may be the quickest way to surface resistance or acceptance. For example, it can assist leaders in knowing whether people need more time to adapt to a change because of a sense of loss or need more support because they are scared.

On a cultural level, North American society, heavily shaped by dominant white, heterosexual, masculine values,[1] favors the cognitive and behavioral dimensions. Value is placed on *right* thinking and *right* action. In US culture, less value has historically been placed on the affective dimension. People who use their feelings to make a decision are thought to be inferior to those who use their cognitive power. They are said to be "swayed by their feelings." No matter how convoluted or inaccurate a person's thinking is, we don't say he was "swayed by this thinking."

Our culture also devalues our affective way of learning and deciding when we say, "Feelings are neither right nor wrong; they just are. It's what we do with them that counts." In other words, how we *behave* takes priority over how we *feel*. I suspect that the intention here is to say that it's okay to be angry, but that it's not okay to hurt someone because of our anger, and so on for other feelings. While I agree that feelings are neither good nor bad, I prefer to talk about them as *congruent* with the stimuli that produce them. But this construction—"Feelings are neither right nor wrong; they just are"—devalues the use of feelings in knowing and transformation. We do not say that that thinking or behaving is neither right nor wrong, that they just are. Feelings give us clues about what we need in a particular situation. Feelings bear messages about how to act ethically toward ourselves and in relation to others. When a feeling is congruent with the stimulus that evoked it, we get a clear message about what is needed. In this way there is something *right* about feelings. The notion of congruence will become clearer in a later chapter in which I talk about the substitution of feelings after reflecting on the six feeling families. In the simplest examples, my feeling awareness and expression are congruent with the stimulus when sad at a loss, scared by what I perceive as dangerous, and angry when my boundaries have been violated or my expectations have been shattered.

Because this book is about becoming emotionally literate (reading our own and other people's feelings accurately) and affectively competent (responding appropriately in groups with full use of the messages that come to us in our feelings), we will be going against the grain of society. We will be acting counter-culturally. The difficulty in becoming emotionally literate is that most of us have been taught to be suspicious of our feelings, to not trust them. The US cultural suspicion of feelings is so pervasive that when we speak of people from cultures that give more respect to feelings, we tend to question those people's ability to think rationally. I believe that built into Western society is a tendency to view thinking as clearer and more important than feeling when it comes to learning and engaging in transformation. Even authors such as Daniel Goleman and his colleagues, who made popular the term *emotional intelligence*, exhibit a bias against the affective dimension. As I read their work, it is about various forms of cognition—thinking. *Emotional* merely modifies intelligence; feelings are subsumed under intelligence and do not stand alongside cognition as an equal partner. For this reason, I prefer to talk about affective *competence* in order to place it on a par with cognitive competence and behavioral competence. That is to say, we learn and we bring about transformation through our thinking, through our feelings, and through our actions or behaviors. All are important, and we can gain competence in all three dimensions. Buying into the dominant cultural bias that cognitive learning and behavioral learning are greater than affective learning is a form of internalized oppression. We may have grown up in a family and a culture that said feelings are less than thinking. When we collude in that hierarchy, we exercise a form of oppression against ourselves.

Another example of the devaluation of feelings can be found in the language sometimes used in 12-step programs. The phrase "feelings are not facts," when used as a mantra, may stop people from drinking, but it carries the danger that people will distrust their feelings rather than bad reasoning. If I feel depressed and the world seems to have turned against me, my habit might be to tell myself, "I'm depressed. A drink or two will make me *feel* better or at least take my mind off my troubles." The problem is *not* the feeling of depression. The problem is the rationalization that alcohol or drugs is the solution. Yet people do not say, "Thoughts are not facts." I believe the goal is to avoid the inaccurate, non*fact*ual conclusion that drinking or drugs or overeating is the solution to "feeling bad" (that is, angry, sad, scared). My point is simply that in the service of a good cause, interrupting addictive behavior, we are told to be suspicious of our feelings or taught to degrade feelings.

While society tends to devalue feelings as compared to cognitive or behavioral approaches to learning and change, individuals may still have a bias or preference for any one of the approaches. Our families of origin also influence our inclination toward or away from one approach or another. Depending on the strength of family pressure and our own personality, we might also conform to the biases of our parents or rebel against them. As a pastor doing premarital counseling, I invited couples to reflect on their approach and whether they were more like one of their parents or the other. Clearly, both parents, if present in one's upbringing, would not necessarily have the same approach. Many clergy use the Myers-Briggs Type Indicator or a shorter inventory developed by David Keirsey and Marilyn Bates for assisting couples in discussing varying personality types, and in particular how they might tend to base their decision making more on thinking or feeling.[2]

I stress these misunderstandings of how feelings work and the devaluation of feelings because I believe the misunderstanding and devaluation get in the way of knowing the full range of our emotional capabilities. My belief is that as we become more comfortable and competent individually and as faith communities in expressing our feelings congruently and reading the feelings of others, we will make better decisions and get more of our intellectual, emotional, and spiritual needs met. The lack of knowledge about how our feelings work and the substitution of feelings into which we have been socially conditioned (for example, expressing sadness when we are really angry) prevent us from bringing about needed changes and from growing as justice-seeking communities.

The first step in becoming more emotionally literate and affectively competent is to swim around in each of the six feeling families. Allow yourself to enter the emotional space of each feeling as it is evoked and described. Feel it in your body. Remember events from your past that the art, poetry, and scripture call to mind. Journal in response to the questions and discuss them with others. After trying on each of the feelings, you can move on to a short discussion of the substitution of feelings and how we sometimes project our feelings onto other people who do not have those feelings. Then we will look at particular applications of the use of feelings in congregational life.

2

Fear

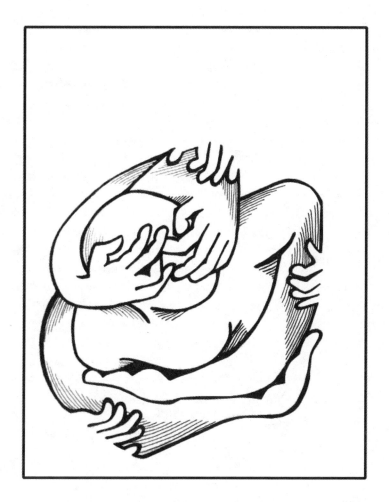

*No passion so effectually robs the mind of all its powers of acting and
reasoning as fear.*
            —*Edmund Burke, 1729–1797* [1]

As you read the poetry and scripture in this chapter, I invite you to be aware of your own fear—perhaps from a childhood experience.

Allow yourself to experience being afraid—to the extent you feel safe doing so. Befriend the discomfort that arises. (If you are a highly anxious person or have had significant trauma in your life, you might want to consult your counselor or trusted confidant before doing this exercise.)

Stop reading at any point to write in a journal or to call a companion to read a passage aloud. Recall your own favorite poems, stories, works of art, and Scripture passages that relate to fear.

As a free writing exercise, write for five minutes beginning with either of these prompts:

> *I am afraid when . . .*
> or
> *Fear is . . .*

Afraid is a country where they issue us passports at birth and hope we never seek citizenship in any other country. The face of afraid keeps changing constantly, and I can count on that change. I need to travel light and fast, and there's a lot of baggage I'm going to have to leave behind me. Jettison cargo.
—*Audre Lorde, "A Burst of Light: Living with Cancer"*[2]

Afraid
You would not sleep either if a man was standing over your bed
    watching you.
He has been there for hours.
He smokes.
I see him through the corner of my arm which hides my face.
I have not moved.
I am waiting for him to stab me.
After a while, I roll over and moan loudly . . . but he does not
    frighten.
He bends over me; then straightens.
I decide to be bold. Roll over again.
Stretch, moan, look at the clock as if he is not there.
I shake out my hair.
I get up, brush by him to the bathroom.

Make noises.
I flush the toilet.
Pretend to return.
But dash instead to the hall.
I go quickly down the carpet to the next room.
Afraid.
The man is not chasing me.
I try the first door. It is open.
I go in.
The room is dark.
Someone is sleeping.
I approach the bed wanting to ask softly for help.
But I am afraid.
What will they think?
I stand over the sleeper watching
After a while, I smoke.
It is a man my age.
His face is hidden by the crook of his elbow.
I do not move when he rolls over and moans loudly.
                                        —*James Carroll* [3]

I Give You Back
I release you, my beautiful and terrible
fear. I release you. You were my beloved
and hated twin, but now, I don't know you
as myself. I release you with all the
pain I would know at the death of
my children.
You are not my blood anymore.
I give you back to the soldiers
who burned down my home, beheaded my children,
raped and sodomized my brothers and sisters.
I give you back to those who stole the food from our plates when
    we were starving.
I release you, fear, because you hold
these scenes in front of me and I was born
with eyes that can never close.
I release you
I release you
I release you
I release you
I am not afraid to be angry,

I am not afraid to rejoice.
I am not afraid to be black.
I am not afraid to be white.
I am not afraid to be hungry.
I am not afraid to be full.
I am not afraid to be hated.
I am not afraid to be loved.
to be loved, to be loved, fear.
Oh, you have choked me, but I gave you the leash.
You have gutted me but I gave you the knife.
You have devoured me, but I laid myself across the fire.
I take myself back, fear.
you are not my shadow any longer.
I won't hold you in my hands.
You can't live in my eyes, my ears, my voice
my belly, or in my heart my heart
my heart my heart
But come here, fear
I am alive and you are so afraid
           of dying.
                 —*Joy Harjo* [4]

Many bulls encircle me,
strong bulls of Bashan surround me;
they open wide their mouths at me,
like a ravening and roaring lion.
I am poured out like water,
and all my bones are out of joint;
my heart is like wax;
it is melted within my breast;
my mouth is dried up like a potsherd,
and my tongue sticks to my jaws;
you lay me in the dust of death.
For dogs are all around me;
a company of evildoers encircles me.
My hands and feet have shriveled;
I can count all my bones.
They stare and gloat over me;
they divide my clothes among themselves,
and for my clothing they cast lots.
                 —*Psalm 22:12–18*

Jesus Stills a Storm

On that day, when evening had come, he said to them, "Let us go across to the other side." And leaving the crowd behind, they took him with them in the boat, just as he was. Other boats were with him. A great windstorm arose, and the waves beat into the boat, so that the boat was already being swamped. But he was in the stern, asleep on the cushion; and they woke him up and said to him, "Teacher, do you not care that we are perishing?" He woke up and rebuked the wind, and said to the sea, "Peace! Be still!" Then the wind ceased, and there was a dead calm. He said to them, "Why are you afraid? Have you still no faith?" And they were filled with great awe and said to one another, "Who then is this, that even the wind and the sea obey him?"

—*Mark 4:35–41*

Jesus Walks on the Water

When evening came, the boat was out on the sea, and he was alone on the land. When he saw that they were straining at the oars against an adverse wind, he came towards them early in the morning, walking on the sea. He intended to pass them by. But when they saw him walking on the sea, they thought it was a ghost and cried out; for they all saw him and were terrified. But immediately he spoke to them and said, "Take heart, it is I; do not be afraid." Then he got into the boat with them and the wind ceased. And they were utterly astounded, for they did not understand about the loaves, but their hearts were hardened.

—*Mark 6:47–52*

A Childhood Fear

When I was probably about nine or ten years old, my father and I went on a fishing trip with his friend Pat and Pat's son Mike. After driving about four hours on highways, we turned off and took a windy road up into the mountains. The last ten or fifteen miles was a narrow dirt road to the area where we set up camp. A few tents and a trailer were in the area. Because it was nearing sunset, the dads asked if Mike and I could set up the tent while they went to get some food for dinner. We were thrilled to be entrusted with making camp and hardly noticed their departure after they unloaded the tent, sleeping gear, camp stove, and lantern. We busied ourselves with setting up the tent and collecting firewood for the campfire. We even used our bowie knives to make shavings for kindling. We were Cub Scouts after all. By the time all was ready, a couple of hours had passed and it was getting pretty dark. The trailer across the way had its lights on. We noticed some fires in pits near a few tents. We were hungry and starting to get a little scared. Where were our dads? The town at the turnoff surely had a store. It wasn't that far away. What was keeping them? A flat tire? Engine trouble? Surely not an accident?

We were getting cold along with tired, hungry, and scared. But we didn't have any matches to start the fire. Finally, we got up enough courage to walk over to the trailer to ask for matches. The folks we'd seen there seemed friendly enough. And looking back, I suspect we sensed our need for some other adults to know our situation.

After a few questions, the couple asked if we wanted to wait for our dads in their trailer. Saying we thought they'd be back soon, we declined. Truth is we didn't want our dads to think we were "little kids" in need of babysitting.

The man from the trailer followed us back to our camp, complimented us on our wood stack, and watched as we lit our fire. He stayed a few minutes and said that we would be welcome back at the trailer if we changed our minds.

The fire calmed us for a while. But as time crawled on, I became scared again, making up stories of terrible things that could have happened. Mike seemed less scared, though some of that might have been a show. When I finally suggested that we go back to the trailer, Mike said he agreed they'd been gone too long, but this had happened to him before. "My dad likes to drink. I'll bet they stopped at a bar."

I don't remember whether I found that reassuring or more worrisome. I didn't have to think about it long, because shortly after that we saw the lights of a car heading our way. Before long

we were eating and telling stories around the fire. What I do remember is that I had trouble falling asleep that night and woke
up from a nightmare, which was not common to my childhood.

I surprised myself when I began to remember this incident. It
has been years since I thought of that trip. The rest of the weekend was really a lot of fun. We caught and ate many fish. The
weather was great. I liked spending time with both my dad and
my buddy, Mike. *And* there was something pretty scary about
that first evening that kept the memory pretty well buried until I
began reading the quotations that open this chapter.

Though I have been ordained for decades, and have preached
hundreds if not thousands of times, I still often feel scared when
I am asked to preach. Sometimes my fear seems mostly about the
content of the sermon. I may have struggled with the scripture
or the topic or the examples, or my own set of beliefs, or even my
relationship with God at that moment in my life. Other times my
fear seems to have more to do with the audience, the congregation.
If I have been asked to be a guest preacher or speaker, I may not
know them and wonder how they will hear what I have to say.
Or perhaps, I know them too well and can anticipate a variety
of responses, some of which I suspect will be negative. Whether
the fear is about the content or the audience, when I am scared,
my emotional response is telling me that some sort of *danger* is
inherent in the situation and that I need *support* or *protection*.

You may be the leader of a committee or a member who has
been asked to research a particular subject and report back to
the group. Your experience tells you this group can be extremely
critical. Even though you know all the members and have a good
relationship with them as individuals outside the meeting, you feel
nervous or scared as the meeting approaches. *Danger* may seem
like too strong a word for what lies ahead, but your *caution* sign
is lit up. It may even be flashing bright yellow.

A little fear or apprehension can be helpful. It can sharpen one's
focus. It can cause us to be more alert and aware. The adrenaline

that is triggered can stimulate us to be ready for what lies ahead and flexible to move in different directions. It can activate us, in extreme circumstances, to be ready for fight or flight.

Being *scared* is a signal. It delivers a message of a real or perceived danger, one that is present or in the near future. Fear invites us to examine whether the danger is real or imagined. If my fear is that no one will listen to what I have to say or that everyone will hate me for presenting my research, the danger of being completely dismissed or utterly disliked may be exaggerated. If I am the treasurer of the congregation and have failed to pay the bills or make timely financial reports for several months, the danger that I might be fired or replaced at the upcoming annual meeting might be very real.

Fear, or the feeling of being scared, makes us aware of a possible danger. The message is to *get safe* or to get protection and support. In the case of a lightning storm, we generally move indoors if we can. If the fear is about the reaction of others to my sermon or my presentation, I might seek support in preparing my data. I might try to find allies, others who can assist in my presentation or who might speak favorably about what I have done. I might rehearse what I have to say with someone I trust to give me helpful critical feedback to improve my odds of being clear, concise, and helpful in what I have to say and how I say it.

The paradigm for fear looks like this:

Stimulus →	**Feeling** →	**Message** →	**Need or Response**
Danger	**SCARED**	I am in danger.	Get safe.
(real or			Get protection
perceived)			and support.

The *afraid* family includes the following: anxious, frightened, bewildered, confused, stressed out, overwhelmed, embarrassed, discouraged, insecure, and submissive. Experiencing dread and being stressed out are relatives of fear or being afraid. Though anxiety is part of this feeling family, psychologists often distinguish anxiety from fear in that the stimulus is harder to isolate. Anxiety often is said to be "free floating," that is, without a specific refer-ent. This makes it harder to name an immediate external threat or to evaluate the level of danger.

The stimulus for feeling afraid is either a *real* danger, such as a powerful person verbally or physically attacking me, or a *perceived* danger, for example, believing I will be unable to pay my mortgage if I don't find a job. The message associated with feeling afraid is "I am in danger." The need I have is to get safe or to arrange for protection or support.

How Fear Shows Up in the Body

The physiological hints that I am afraid include the following: increase in heart rate, a tightness in my chest or stomach or some-times throat. I can also experience sweating more than normal, a shortness of breath, shaking or trembling, dryness in my mouth, or difficulty swallowing. My skin may turn pale. These symptoms vary in degree and from person to person. By tracking your physi-cal responses at times you know you are afraid, you can use these symptoms as clues during times when you are not sure what you might be feeling.

Fear and Connection

While it is true that extreme fear might lead someone to with-draw into isolation, to disappear from relationships, the impetus of fear is such that it causes one to seek support, to connect with those who can provide safety or protection. As is the case with other emotions, fear does not turn us only in upon ourselves. Its communal nature invites connection that is helpful, that provides assurance, help in building skills, and a reality check if we are ex-aggerating the perceived danger. In healthy adult relationships, we move in and out of the roles of giving and receiving help, protection, and support. When we mentor others who have less experience than we have, we may provide the greater share of support because that is what we have agreed to. At the same time, if we are in a position of authority or are in a group (for example, white, male, or clergy) that historically has had more authority or privilege than the person who is scared, then we need to be careful that our behavior does not become, or is not perceived as, *dysfunctional rescuing*, which is linked to a person in power acting as though they are better than or smarter than the person they are attempting to help.[5]

Fear and Gender

What one fears probably mostly has to do with the circumstances of how one was raised. Some people fear being alone; others are more afraid in a large crowd. Some of us fear the limelight; others fear not being noticed at all. Some people are nervous in uncertain situations; others like the challenge of change and are afraid of becoming bored by routine. While personality or social conditioning may account for some of these differences, the former is too specific and the latter too general to help us engage in discussions about how we can learn from one another about fear and support each other when fear arises. While I recognize the importance of exercising a great deal of caution about generalizing, I have been fascinated by differences that men and women report about their fears in relationships.[6]

Relational-cultural theorists and playwrights Stephen Bergman and Janet Surrey suggest that in relationships, women are more likely to fear loss of connection or separation, while men are more likely to fear loss of independence or autonomy. Berman calls this *male relational dread*. For some men, the invitation to deeper connection, a curiosity by a female partner about what he feels, is experienced as criticism of his competence or his style of interaction. In circumstances where this invitation is recurrent, the man experiences it as something that will get out of control to the point that he is in danger of losing his very soul. At the same time, the female partner might yearn for deeper connection and fear the male companion will withdraw from connection. This sometimes leads the woman to lower her expectations of deeper connection for fear of scaring him off. She withdraws a part of herself from the relationship. She decides not to show up as her full self in order to maintain what she can of the relationship. The dance of differing expectations and fears is referred to by Surrey and Bergman as the dread/yearning impasse.[7] Their conclusion is not that men do not have feelings, but rather that they need more time and space to process their feelings, because they have historically had less cultural support to acknowledge and attend to their feelings, with the exception that they have had cultural support to feel and express anger.

Shelley E. Taylor, a psychology professor at UCLA and leading researcher on stress and gender, has proposed along with five colleagues that women *tend* and *befriend* in stressful (fearful) situations. This response is distinct from the more typical *fight-or-flight* response of men, which was the dominant fear paradigm until their research in the late 1990s. In particular, women respond to stressful situations "by protecting themselves and their young through nurturing behaviors" (*tending*) and "forming alliances with a larger social group, particularly among women" (*befriending*). Women "show the same immediate hormonal and sympathetic nervous system response to acute stress"; then, building on the brain's attachment and care-giving system, women's bodies tend to counteract the metabolic activity associated with the fight-or-flight stress response—increased heart rate, blood pressure, and cortisone levels—and respond with tending-and-befriending behaviors.[8] Researchers postulate that fleeing too rapidly at any sign of danger would put the female's offspring at risk, thereby reducing her reproductive success in evolutionary terms. Studies in female rats in stressful situations have shown the release of oxytocin, which enhances relaxation, reduces fearfulness, and mitigates the typical fight-or-flight responses. Taylor's continuing research in this area led to the publication of *The Tending Instinct: How Nurturing Is Essential to Who We Are and How We Live*, in which she writes, "The difference between women's and men's inclination to turn to the social group in times of stress ranks with 'giving birth' as among the most reliable sex differences there are."[9]

Fear and Growth

The Indian social activist and spiritual teacher Vimala Thakar (1921–2009) speaks of the vulnerability that lies behind fear and that enables us to grow.

> When there is no fear of living and no fear of dying, we can realize our potential for growth.
>
> We would like the river of life to move as the calm waters of a protected canal; we don't want the river to thrust us into the mainstream with rapids and white water, exposed, vulnerable.
>
> But vulnerability has a beauty, a significance.
>
> It is only when we are willing to be vulnerable, unprotected by fixed ideas, traditions, and habitual ways, that the adventure of self-discovery, the inward voyage can begin.[10]

Thakar's focus is on the inner journey of self-discovery. She spent more than four decades teaching meditation and philosophy.

Actors and preachers also experience vulnerability that can lead to connection with others. They speak of "stage fright." In its extreme form, it can paralyze the speaker. Its milder form seems to provide the energy (through adrenaline) to rise to the occasion or to keep the speaker on her toes. Here the vulnerability opens the speaker up to experiencing how the audience perceives her. She is more alert and flexible. The speaker's vulnerability leads her to seek support in the form of feedback from the audience in order to become more adept at accomplishing her task of communication.

Fear and Power

The quotation from Audre Lorde that opens this chapter illustrates the way fear can be used as a tool in the hands of a dominant group to keep others in their subordinate places. Perhaps the cargo that Lorde invites us to jettison is the notion that we are inferior and that others are superior. That certainly requires a new way of living—a dramatic change personally, institutionally, and culturally. If we can be convinced to live in the country of fear, to never leave, then the systems of injustice and oppression will remain as they are. One benefit of affective competency is that when we begin to pay closer attention to our feelings, we see how they can become tools for liberation. Our fear can remind us that we need allies and colleagues for protection and support.

One of my most significant memories as a young adult is participating with farmworkers in La Causa—the struggle of farmworkers for healthy living conditions and better wages. I remember the transformation I saw in individual workers from being fearful to feeling powerful. These largely "undocumented" laborers were issued fear passports, often by their own jefes (bosses), in order to keep them in check—that is, submissive to low wages and unsafe working conditions. The farmworkers were right to be afraid of those wielding power over them. There was a very real danger that they would be deported or beaten. The United Farm Workers, together with the AFL-CIO, also employed power, but of a different sort. They employed *power with*. They heard within the emotion of fear a message that the way out of danger was to enlist union members and normal citizens as allies in the struggle for justice. What started as a small strike in the vineyards of Delano, California, became an international boycott of grapes, including the cooperation of longshoremen who refused to unload foreign grapes. Two years after the boycott began, California grape growers agreed to the first farm labor contracts.

Fearful Communities

Organizational development literature, including books on congregational leadership and how congregations function as systems, have discussed the role of anxiety in congregations.[11] In *Congregational Resources for Facing Feelings*, you will find examples of how fear operates in various pastoral contexts. The point here is to notice that in the same way an individual may have a primary affective orientation, so also a congregation may have a predominant affective stance from which it operates.

A colleague and I once did several months of consulting and training for lay and clergy leaders from four small struggling congregations that had received a grant to see what they could learn together in order to support each other, perhaps even developing some shared ministries. The demographics with regard to age, race, denomination, size, and suburban location were very similar. Each congregation had a clergyperson who was employed only part time by the congregation. They seemed pretty much the same to each other and to the consultants until we did an exercise in which the leaders were encouraged to talk about which primary feeling was most allowed and which was least allowed in their congregation. As the exercise unfolded, it became clear that there were two *scared* congregations, one *sad* congregation, and one congregation that identified primarily as *powerful*. At that moment the participants from all the congregations as well as the trainers had a major "Aha!" The congregations had joined together to write a grant to fund their training and work with two consultants, and they were "deeply committed to working together on ministries and develop a sensible economy of scale for administrative and education projects." Yet despite their best intentions, they did not seem to gel. They had trouble understanding one another. Then it became obvious: despite similar membership and financial problems, the work each congregation had to do was quite different from an *affective* point of view. It also made sense that the leaders from the two *scared* congregations felt most *sympatico*.

As is the case with individuals, fear is not to be seen as a negative emotion in groups. Corporate anxiety can lead people to assess the reality of the perceived danger. When a congregation is continuing to spend its endowment at a rate that will lead to its extinction and failing to consider other avenues to gain financial viability, a healthy dose of fear might be warranted. Corporate fear can be a wake-up call for finding functional support. Ronald Heifetz, Senior Lecturer in Public Leadership and cofounder of the Center for Public Leadership at the John F. Kennedy School of Government at Harvard University, speaks of the need to turn up the heat high enough in a situation to get things cooking, without boiling the pot over. Sometimes fear is the fuel or catalyst that allows the right amount of pressure for necessary change to take place.

Resources

Friedman, Edwin. *Generation to Generation: Family Process in Church and Synagogue.* New York: Guildford Press, 1985, and *A Failure of Nerve: Leadership in the Age of the Quick Fix,* edited by Margaret M. Treadwell and Edward W. Beal. New York: Seabury Books, 2007, published posthumously. Friedman was a leader in bringing the work of family systems theorists, particularly Murray Bowen, into congregational discussions.

Heifetz, Ronald A., and Marty Linsky. *Leadership on the Line: Staying Alive through the Dangers of Leading.* Cambridge, MA: Harvard Business School Press, 2002. Ronald Heifetz, Alexander Grashow, and Marty Linsky. *The Practice of Adaptive Leadership: Tools and Tactics for Changing Your Organization and the World.* Boston: Harvard Business Press, 2009. These authors look at the roles of leaders within systems. They are best known for the distinction between *technical fixes* (for which experts have the answers) and *adaptive challenges* (which require new learning and deeper collaboration between those with the problem and outside experts).

Kehoe, Nancy. *Wrestling with Our Inner Angels: Faith, Mental Illness, and the Journey to Wholeness.* San Francisco: Jossey-Bass, 2009. As a psychologist and Roman Catholic nun, Kehoe tells stories of how she changed and grew through leading religious issues groups in locked wards. She argues against the view that religion only adds to the problems of those diagnosed with mental illness.

Lerner, Harriet. *The Dance of Fear: Rising above Anxiety, Fear, and Shame to Be Your Best and Bravest Self.* New York: Harper, 2004. First published as *Fear and Other Uninvited Guests,* the book covers common fears such as rejection, anxiety, change, the workplace, looks, and life when things fall apart.

Steinke, Peter L. *Congregational Leadership in Anxious Times: Being Calm and Courageous No Matter What.* Herndon, VA: Alban Institute, 2006. Steinke draws upon systems theory to help leaders understand their roles in congregations.

Reflection Questions

Personal Level

1. What are you afraid of?
2. What wakes you up at night and won't let you go back to sleep?
3. Is the danger that you fear real or imagined? Whom can you talk with to get a reality check about the degree of danger or its imminence?
4. If the danger is real, where might you go to avoid or lessen the danger? (For example, the danger of a violent, abusive spouse or partner might require relocating to a safe house or to another state. Similarly, some laypeople and clergy find a particular congregation to be toxic or abusive.)
5. Whom might you turn to for protection or support? How might you proceed so that this support does not lead you to feel inferior, such that it leads to a sense of helplessness?

Congregational Level

1. Where do people experience fear or anxiety on a corporate level in your congregation?
2. What dangers pose a threat to your congregation?
3. How might you be in danger of losing your soul or your uniqueness as a congregation?
4. Where do you find your greatest support as a people? Name some instances when you looked to your founders or ancestors as models of flexibility or courage in times of danger or periods of instability or rapid change.

5. Who is the God you believe in most right now? God who is your rock and your sure foundation? A redeemer or rescuer God? One who leads you out of the wilderness? Christ who dies, rises, and ascends but who leaves behind the Spirit who will teach you all things?
6. Which specific individuals can you count on during your time of terror? How might you elicit their commitment?
7. What are you willing to put forward by way of support at this time?

3
Anger

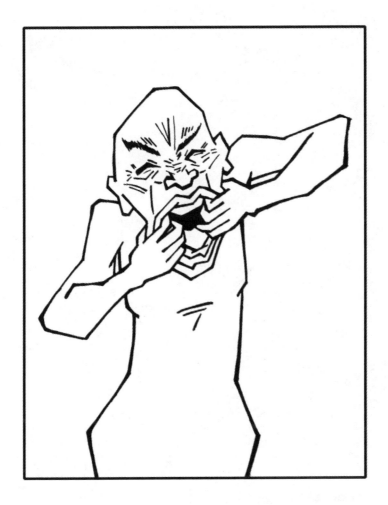

But who is man that is not angry?
—William Shakespeare, 1564–1616, Timon of Athens [1]

As you read the poetry and scripture in this chapter, I invite you to be aware of your own anger—when your boundaries have been crossed or when your expectations have been shattered. You may also remember times of anger that do not seem to be anchored in any particular event.

1. Allow yourself to experience your anger. Befriend the feelings that arise.
2. Stop reading at any point to write in a journal or to call a companion to read a passage aloud. Recall your own favorite poems, stories, and Scripture passages that relate to sadness.
3. As a free writing exercise, write for five minutes beginning with either of these prompts:

I am angry when . . .
or
Anger is . . .

Anger is not the opposite of love. It is better understood as a feeling-signal that all is not well in our relation to other persons or groups or to the world around us. . . . To put the point another way: anger is—and it always is—a sign of some resistance in ourselves to the moral quality of the social relations in which we are immersed. Extreme and intense anger signals a deep reaction to the action upon us or toward others to whom we are related. . . . Such anger is a signal that change is called for, that transformation in relation is required.

—*Beverly Wildung Harrison,*
"The Power of Anger in the Work of Love"[2]

A man that does not know how to be angry does not know how to be good. Now and then a man should be shaken to the core with indignation over things evil.

—*Henry Ward Beecher, 1813–87,*
Proverbs from Plymouth Pulpit[3]

My tongue will tell the anger of my heart
Or else my heart, concealing it, will break,

And, rather than it shall, I will be free
Even to the uttermost, as I please, in words.
                    —*William Shakespeare, 1564–1616,*
                        The Taming of the Shrew [4]

⌣

Hot indignation seizes me because of the wicked,
those who forsake your law.
                    —*Psalm 119:53*

⌣

Again he entered the synagogue, and a man was there who had a
withered hand. They watched him to see whether he would cure
him on the sabbath, so that they might accuse him. And he said to
the man who had the withered hand, "Come forward." Then he
said to them, "Is it lawful to do good or to do harm on the sabbath, to save life or to kill?" But they were silent. He looked around
at them with anger; he was grieved at their hardness of heart and
said to the man, "Stretch out your hand." He stretched it out, and
his hand was restored. The Pharisees went out and immediately
conspired with the Herodians against him, how to destroy him.
                    —*Mark 3:1–6*

⌣

So then, putting away falsehood, let all of us speak the truth to
our neighbors, for we are members of one another. Be angry but
do not sin; do not let the sun go down on your anger, and do not
make room for the devil. Thieves must give up stealing; rather let
them labor and work honestly with their own hands, so as to have
something to share with the needy.
                    —*Ephesians 4:25–28*

⌣

The Passover of the Jews was near, and Jesus went up to Jerusalem.
In the temple he found people selling cattle, sheep, and doves, and
the money changers seated at their tables. Making a whip of cords,
he drove all of them out of the temple, both the sheep and the
cattle. He also poured out the coins of the money changers and
overturned their tables. He told those who were selling the doves,
"Take these things out of here! Stop making my Father's house a
marketplace!" His disciples remembered that it was written, "Zeal
for your house will consume me."
                    —*John 2:13–17*

The LORD passed before him, and proclaimed, "The LORD, the LORD, a God merciful and gracious, slow to anger, and abounding in steadfast love and faithfulness, keeping steadfast love for the thousandth generation, forgiving iniquity and transgression and sin, yet by no means clearing the guilty, but visiting the iniquity of the parents upon the children and the children's children, to the third and the fourth generation." And Moses quickly bowed his head toward the earth, and worshiped. He said, "If now I have found favor in your sight, O Lord, I pray, let the Lord go with us. Although this is a stiff-necked people, pardon our iniquity and our sin, and take us for your inheritance."
—*Exodus 34:6–9*

Yet he, being compassionate,
forgave their iniquity,
and did not destroy them;
often he restrained his anger,
and did not stir up all his wrath.
—*Psalm 78:38*

Reclaiming Anger

Perhaps more than any other emotion, anger gets a bad rap. We can deal with a sad relative or friend, as long as they are not sad for too long. We usually do okay with someone who is afraid, even if we do not find the source of their fear compelling. But most of us would prefer not to be around any angry person, especially if the anger is directed toward us.

Anger is nearly always presented as a *negative* emotion—something to be controlled, stifled, kept in check, converted to something else. This damage-control approach to anger may be best summed up by Aristotle, who wrote:

Anyone can get angry—that is easy—or give or spend money; but to do this to the right person, to the right extent, at the right time, with the right aim, and in the right way, *that* is not for everyone, nor is it easy.[5]

Unlike many contemporary authors, Aristotle at least admits to a right time and purpose for anger. What is more common, for both biblical and secular writers, is to see anger leading to evil or becoming harmful to the one who is angry. Take, for example, the following quotations:

> Refrain from anger, and forsake wrath. Do not fret—it leads only to evil.
>
> —Psalm 37:8

> Anger's my meat; I sup upon myself,
> And so shall starve with feeding.
> —William Shakespeare, 1564–1616, *Coriolanus*[6]

> Of the Seven Deadly Sins, anger is possibly the most fun. To lick your wounds, to smack your lips over grievances long past, to roll over your tongue the prospect of bitter confrontations still to come, to savor to the last toothsome morsel both the pain you are given and the pain you are giving back—in many ways it is a feast fit for a king. The chief drawback is that what you are wolfing down is yourself. The skeleton at the feast is you.
> —Frederick Buechner, *Wishful Thinking*[7]

Despite the fact that Jesus himself was angry on a number of occasions, most Christians find it very difficult to have a positive understanding of anger. Even for those who distinguish between holy or righteous anger and unrighteous anger, anger mostly falls into the latter category. For this reason, hundreds of books have been written on how to control anger. Daylong and weeklong workshops and Internet seminars on dealing with one's anger abound. Anger management is a multimillion-dollar cottage industry.

I want to be clear that I support all efforts to reduce and eliminate abusive and violent behaviors in which people—usually men or others who are in a dominant or power-over relationship—often engage. But the problem, as I see it, is not the emotion of anger but the imbalance of power and the use of violence to maintain, or at times to attempt to rebalance, that power.

I would suggest a different starting point for viewing anger and rescuing it from the scrap heap of discarded or unwanted emotions. Anger is a naturally occurring emotion. According to Thomas Fuller, the early seventeenth-century English churchman and historian, it is "one of the sinews of the soul."[8] A sinew is a tough, fibrous tissue that connects bone to bone or muscle to bone. Imagine if we thought of anger as a tough connective tissue that unites us within ourselves, to God, and to others![9] Might there be a way that anger holds us together, binding us to our most cherished values, our deepest beliefs, our truest desires? How would our lives change if anger functioned to link us more deeply to the Holy One and to other people?

The schematic of anger looks like this:

Stimulus →	Feeling →	Message →	Need or Response
Violation (real or perceived)	**ANGRY (MAD)**	I have been violated. My expectations have been shattered.	Renegotiate boundaries. Renegotiate expectations.

The feeling of anger arises naturally within us when we or someone we care about has been violated, been abused, or met with an injustice. The feeling arises when our boundaries have been violated or our expectations have been shattered. Anger is the affective clue that we are disconnected from God, from ourselves, from right relationship with other people. Sometimes, we describe this affective response more as a *discomfort* with what is happening or a *disappointment* about what ought to be happening but is not. Anger can be felt as the pinprick of conscience that says something is not right here, a relationship is in need of transformation or restoration. Beverly Wildung Harrison, the first woman president of the North American Society of Christian Ethics, speaks about the relationship of anger to community:

We need to recognize that where the evasion of feeling is widespread, anger does not go away or disappear. Rather, in interpersonal life it masks itself as boredom, ennui, low energy, or it expresses itself in passive-aggressive activity or in moralistic self-righteousness and blaming. Anger denied subverts community. Anger expressed directly is a mode of taking the other seriously, of caring. The important point is that where feeling is evaded, where anger is hidden or goes unattended, masking itself, there the power of love, the power to act, to deepen relation, atrophies and dies.[10]

How Anger Shows Up in the Body

When cartoon characters get angry, steam comes out of their ears. Their heads seem to swell as they turn red and utter loud, explosive words. In common speech we talk about getting "hot under the collar." In reality, your heartbeat may increase by eight beats per minute and your body temperature does rise. Hair may stand on end and breathing may be uneven or jerky. You may experience a sudden tension in your fists, arms, neck, or shoulders or the onset of sweating or a headache. Some people quickly become hyperactive; others go into a slow burn or seethe quietly. Women may describe the onset of anger as slowly building; men may describe it as a fire or a raging flood. Women may release oxytocin and men more adrenaline and noradrenaline. The amygdala, the part of the brain that deals with emotion, can become highly active within a quarter of a second. At the same time, blood flow increases to the frontal lobe, the portion of the brain over the left eye that controls reasoning and tends to moderate a sudden overreaction, such as taking a swing at someone or throwing the nearest ashtray. Because this balancing neurological response occurs within two seconds, counting to ten when angry is wise advice. When the nervous system is continually stressed in someone with frequent bouts of anger, the heart may be weakened, blood pressure may rise, arteries may stiffen, and the liver and kidneys can suffer damage. Some scientists believe chronic anger may be more dangerous to health than either smoking or obesity. For this reason, it is important to understand how anger's message about renegotiating boundaries and expectations mitigates the physical effects of prolonged anger that does not engage in seeking remedies.

Anger and Connection

Anger, like all emotions, is not simply a private experience that one feels. Anger links us to others. You have probably heard someone say that they get mad only at people or situations they care about. As one who frequently takes my life in my hands by driving in Boston, I have reservations about agreeing completely! There are people who are complete strangers to me with whom I become very angry when their driving is utterly rude or randomly careless. Nevertheless, I am aware that most of the time, it is people I really care about who stimulate my anger. And the feeling of anger that arises is a signal to me that our connection to one another is broken or frayed or in danger of becoming so. With the people to whom I am closest, anger is not an obstacle to connection but rather an invitation to examine the quality of the connection and a summons to investigate the values we hold. Frequently for me, my anger is a sign that I need a little more space from the other person or time to process what is taking place. Unfortunately, rather than stating that need, I lash out or become prickly in such a way as to cause the other person to back off—creating the distance I wanted or needed. At other times the anger is because I had expectations that were not met. Perhaps I assumed my partner would arrive earlier than she did, or I presumed the report I asked for would be more detailed.

Anger and Gender

Anger does not follow equal opportunity guidelines. That is to say, those of us who identify as male and those of us who identify as female have been socialized differently with regard to *whether* and *how* we are allowed to express anger. Generally speaking in North America, men, and particularly white men, have the greatest permission to feel and express anger. In certain circumstances, men who are angry are seen as assertive or strong; women in similar situations are perceived as aggressive or "bitchy." While this generalization is in part about the way men and women are allowed to *behave* when they are feeling angry, there is also truth to the fact that the messages boys and girls are given from an early age affect what we come to believe we have permission to feel. Often when working with groups, I have heard women say they were not permitted to even feel anger; and while men will say they were allowed to feel anger, the message to them was about how much or how little they could act on or express their anger, with permission for greater expression growing as they got older.

Anger and Power

When a person has a great deal of privilege and is able to exercise significant dominance within a system, that person generally is granted, or assumes, the right to freely express his anger. And when the ability to express anger is unequally distributed within a system, it feels oppressive to those with less permission or ability. It takes a great deal of courage to rebalance the system so that all participants have more equal power and similar opportunities to feel and express the entire range of feelings. Perhaps more than with any other feeling, finding allies for the expression of anger is important if you live or work in a system where your ability to notice and express your anger has been stifled.

Angry Communities

One of the most common examples of an angry church system is the "after-pastor" congregation. Congregations are so named when an abuse of authority in the form of sexual or financial misconduct has occurred.[11] Anger can become a central, prevailing emotion in these congregations, because boundaries and expectations have been violated, and the anger is telling members that healthy boundaries need to be reestablished and expectations need to be renegotiated.

I find it helpful to think of a LOYALTY ←—→ ACCOUNTABILITY continuum in congregations. In after-pastor congregations, the discourse has shifted toward loyalty, often toward the far end of the spectrum. Frequently the abuser and his supporters are heard to say, "Don't you trust me (him)?" or "Where's your loyalty?" I remember being in a case-study support group of after-pastors in which one member spoke of the congregation where he served as the interim after-pastor while the former pastor was on trial for alleged sexual misconduct with seventeen female parishioners. The congregation was split between those people *loyal* to the charismatic, talented pastor of twenty-five-plus years, and those people *loyal* to the seventeen women who had accused him of misconduct. The interim believed that a major part of his work was to move members of the congregation to the *accountability* end of the continuum so that the discussion could address a couple of important questions: How can we hold our clergy accountable to healthy emotional and physical boundaries? How might we be more accountable to one another in choosing mature and stable leaders and in responding to early indications that such boundaries are being tested or crossed?

At times, the abuse of authority is not expressed in sexual or financial misconduct but takes the form of prolonged emotional abuse or bullying. I'd like to suggest that the issue here is not anger (as I have described it) but rather shame and blame. (See chapter 9.) In such situations, the shaming and blaming generally originate with a person in authority. At some point, the inappropriate behavior of the abuser infects the system, and others also begin to act in shaming and blaming ways. Because no action is taken to set appropriate behavioral guidelines or to enforce them for the person at the top, the system breaks down. Sometimes this becomes evident only when the abuser has been exposed in a civil or ecclesial action that asserts a violation of appropriate conduct.

Other times, the signs that the system is in trouble appear when board or committee members personally attack one another and no one steps up to suggest a return to civil discourse that rules out shaming and blaming of those with whom one might disagree.

Although I will discuss *shame* briefly in a subsequent chapter, the important point here is that anger invites us to renegotiate boundaries and expectations. This means that all parties need to be accountable for assumptions, expectations, procedures, and boundaries. Anger is a warning sign that something is amiss in these areas. Shame is more aligned with the loyalty end of the spectrum. When people are asking about our loyalty, they are frequently saying we *are* wrong (not just that we have *done* something wrong) and therefore deserving of shame. While loyalty sounds like a virtue, it is a trap when accountability for appropriate behavior is not also part of the system. Another clue that loyalty is a diversion is when those in power require or request loyalty so that they can maintain their power to continue to exercise abuse. Most often those with less power are asking for accountability in order to move toward more equality and transparence.

Resources

The Arbinger Institute. *Leadership and Self-Deception: Getting Out of the Box.* 2002. Reprint, San Francisco: Berrett-Koehler, 2010. In the Ellis tradition, though without acknowledgment, this book tells the story of an executive facing challenges at home and at work, and in so doing demonstrates the psychological processes that conceal our motivations and assumptions from us and thereby trap us in a box of recurring and deepening self-justification. At each step of the cycle, alternatives are offered.

Ellis, Albert. *Anger: How to Live With and Without It.* 1974. Reprint, Secaucus, NJ: Citadel Press, 2002). Ellis, founder of the Institute for Rational-Emotive Therapy (RET) and author of more than forty-five books, posits that our response to any given event is conditioned by our irrational beliefs. He encourages identifying those beliefs and countering them with rational statements

resulting in more appropriate responses—"thinking your way out
of your anger." While overly rational or cognitive, this book (and
RET in general) is useful in pointing out the ways in which we
deceive ourselves by clinging to certain irrational assumptions.

Gaede, Beth, ed. *When a Congregation Is Betrayed: Responding to
Clergy Misconduct.* Herndon, VA: Alban Institute, 2006. A collection of essays by experts in the area of clergy misconduct and its
effect on congregations, this book deals with the initial response
to the misconduct, models for understanding what happened,
roles and responsibilities of various parties as they respond, creating safer congregations, and looking to the future. Incredibly
helpful, practical advice in the wake of the anger, fear, and grief
that congregations face in the wake of misconduct by clergy or lay
leaders.

Hanh, Thich Nhat. *Anger: Wisdom for Cooling the Flames.* New York:
Riverhead Books, 2001. The author, a Vietnamese monk and
teacher, suggests that we are responsible for alleviating our own
suffering caused by anger through mindfulness. We are not to
fight our anger or to "let it all out," which may rehearse our anger
rather than release it. He writes about interpersonal anger as well
as anger between countries and between citizens and govern-
ments. Appendices include meditations and relaxation guides.

Keizer, Garret. *The Enigma of Anger: Essays on a Sometimes Deadly
Sin.* San Francisco: Jossey-Bass, 2004. An Episcopal priest, Keizer
confesses he is "a descendant of angry men" and personally
addresses when unwarranted anger begs forgiveness and when
legitimate anger has a place in Christian life, as well as when it
may mask grief.

Lerner, Harriet. *The Dance of Anger: A Woman's Guide to Changing
the Patterns of Intimate Relationships.* 1985. Reprinted with new
introduction, New York: Harper, 2005. Lerner, a staff psychologist at the Menninger clinic for two decades, suggests that we
focus on ourselves, not others, in order to move out of counter-
productive patterns or dances of anger, even as we stay connected
to others and act with integrity. She talks about the effect this
has on others and how to maintain oneself in the face of counter-
moves.

Tavris, Carol. *Anger: The Misunderstood Emotion*. 1982. Reprint, New York: Simon and Schuster, 1989). As a social psychologist, Tavris has studied anger. She writes about the myths of expressing anger and differences between men and women in expressing anger. She stresses the need to explore within ourselves what triggers our anger.

Reflection Questions

Personal Level

1. When you were growing up, who had the most permission to be angry in your family?
2. As a child, were you allowed to express anger? If so, to whom or with whom were you able to be angry? What sorts of things were you angry about—whether or not you were granted permission to express your anger?
3. What did you do when you were angry and it was not okay to express that anger?
4. Think of the last time you were really angry. Make note of the details of the situation.
5. With whom were you angry?
6. What were you angry about? Was a boundary violated? If so, what line was crossed?
7. Did you have an expectation that was not met? What was your expectation?
8. How did other people know you were angry?
9. What did you do when you were angry and it was not okay to express that anger?

Congregational Level

1. Do members of your congregation ever express anger? If so, what things are members of your congregation angry about?
2. What is the response when people in the congregation say they are angry?

3. Can the pastor, choir director, Sunday school superinten-
   dent, or teachers express anger?
4. How are differences in expectations negotiated?
5. Does your congregation have any history of physical,
   sexual, emotional, or financial abuse by someone in
   authority (clergyperson, treasurer, choir director, educational leader)?

Chapter 4

Sadness

For all sad words of tongue and pen, the saddest are these, "It might have been."
—John Greenleaf Whittier, 1807–1892, Maud Muller [1]

As you read the poetry and scripture in this chapter, I invite you to be aware of your own sadness—over losses you have experienced or that you anticipate. You may also remember times of sadness or grief that do not seem to be anchored in any particular event.

Allow yourself to abide in your sadness. Befriend the feelings that arise.

Stop reading at any point to write in a journal or to call a companion to read a passage aloud. Recall your own favorite poems, stories, and Scripture passages that relate to sadness.

As a free writing exercise, write for five minutes beginning with one of the following prompts:

> *I am sad when . . .*
> or
> *Sadness is . . .*

letting go in autumn
I will
no longer wait
for you to
return my love
you
and your quiet
stealing of breath by
moonlight,
your feeble stealing
of day by lying,
will not be
carried into the
new season.
autumn comes and
with its arrival demands
a new leaf. green
gives way to brownorangeyellowred
brittle leaves
aching to fall off their trees.
their time to die is now.
they understand this; but we
do not.
we stand in dying's way

silently scream as it pulls
what it needs
from us: the ever
receding
light
of truth.
and leaves
in its place, the dull
greyness of only
existing
because we could not let go.
we held on to
yesterday's joy. held on
in fear of never
knowing joy again,
in fear
we would never
find a new laugh to
paint our faces
the colour of summer
to shade us
the rhythm of
rain on rooftops.
we don't know
what music
sounds like any more; we have
forgotten its tone and pitch.
now our walk sings
somber songs of loss longing and
wistful waiting.
the hunger has returned, perpetual hunger never to be fulfilled.
there is no thirst here . . .
that too we have forgotten.
I will
no longer wait
for you to
return my love
the autumn
is here
and like those brittle leaves
I ache to
let go

—Toni Stuart [2]

Grief
Grief is not rational
Grief is you out of control
Grief couldn't care less
About your calendar
Your feeble projections
Based on theories about time
Grief pulls your strings
After letting you loose long enough
To feel the weight of another fall
Grief calls you inside
Locks you up
Takes you back to childish threats and tantrums
None of which make any difference
To what happened
To what is
To what can ever be replaced
Or ever be the same
Grief knows your secret weaknesses
Your hiding places
Can turn the most ordinary, familiar places
Into alien landscapes
Grief will change your walk, your talk
Will bring you unexpectedly to your knees
Grief ignores all your pleas
For relief
Escape
The numb of forgetting
Grief attacks out of the blue
Before you can even think of a defense
And even though you were there
For the brutal digging and carving of this wound
The cruel abruptness of this loss
Grief will make you zone out
Wonder where you are
Puzzle at the smallest and simplest of questions
Grief will make you want to hurt yourself
Will want to hold you back
When time pushes you forward
It will make you think you are stagnant, stuck
Frozen in its grip
Never to be released

Grief will try to convince you
That nothing and no-one can take its place
Grief will pretend to disappear
Then jump up in your face
Laughing at you for thinking
You'd left it behind
Grief teaches you patience
Gives you no choice
Makes you want to rant and howl
Takes away your voice
Grief can destroy all you have built
And believed in
If you let it
If you forget to give in
To realize that resistance
Encourages grief to stay longer
That denial
Invites grief to sink deeper roots
Widen the spread of its blinding poison
Grief is a cleansing fire
Embrace it
Surrender to its demands
Grief knows the way
Knows the only way out
Is through
It is within this cave
Under the spell of its darkness
That grief's real work begins
There
Where we are most afraid to go
there it waits
After the wars of mind and heart
To welcome you
To reveal the truth of its purpose
To grace you with its many gifts
                    —*Malika Ndlovu* [3]

My Soul Is Dark
My soul is dark—Oh! quickly string
The harp I yet can brook to hear;
And let thy gentle fingers fling

Its melting murmurs o'er mine ear.
If in this heart a hope be dear,
That sound shall charm it forth again:
If in these eyes there lurk a tear,
'Twill flow, and cease to burn my brain.
But bid the strain be wild and deep,
Nor let thy notes of joy be first:
I tell thee, minstrel, I must weep,
Or else this heavy heart will burst;
For it hath been by sorrow nursed,
And ached in sleepless silence, long;
And now 'tis doomed to know the worst,
And break at once—or yield to song.

—*Lord Byron, 1788–1824*[4]

For everything there is a season, and a time for every matter under
    heaven:
a time to be born, and a time to die;
a time to plant, and a time to pluck up what is planted;
a time to kill, and a time to heal;
a time to break down, and a time to build up;
a time to weep, and a time to laugh;
a time to mourn, and a time to dance;
a time to throw away stones, and a time to gather stones together;
a time to embrace, and a time to refrain from embracing;
a time to seek, and a time to lose;
a time to keep, and a time to throw away;
a time to tear, and a time to sew;
a time to keep silence, and a time to speak;
a time to love, and a time to hate;
a time for war, and a time for peace.

—*Ecclesiastes 3:1–8*

By the rivers of Babylon—
there we sat down and there we wept
when we remembered Zion.
On the willows there
we hung up our harps.
For there our captors

asked us for songs,
and our tormentors asked for mirth, saying,
"Sing us one of the songs of Zion!"
How could we sing the LORD's song
in a foreign land?
If I forget you, O Jerusalem,
let my right hand wither!
Let my tongue cling to the roof of my mouth,
if I do not remember you,
if I do not set Jerusalem
above my highest joy.
                                    —*Psalm 137:1–6*

When she had said this, she went back and called her sister Mary, and told her privately, "The Teacher is here and is calling for you." And when she heard it, she got up quickly and went to him. Now Jesus had not yet come to the village, but was still at the place where Martha had met him. The Jews who were with her in the house, consoling her, saw Mary get up quickly and go out. They followed her because they thought that she was going to the tomb to weep there. When Mary came where Jesus was and saw him, she knelt at his feet and said to him, "Lord, if you had been here, my brother would not have died." When Jesus saw her weeping, and the Jews who came with her also weeping, he was greatly disturbed in spirit and deeply moved. He said, "Where have you laid him?" They said to him, "Lord, come and see." Jesus began to weep. So the Jews said, "See how he loved him!"
                                    —*John 11:28–36*

As he came near and saw the city, he wept over it.
                                    —*Luke 19:41*

But Mary stood weeping outside the tomb. As she wept, she bent over to look into the tomb; and she saw two angels in white, sitting where the body of Jesus had been lying, one at the head and the other at the feet. They said to her, "Woman, why are you weeping?" She said to them, "They have taken away my Lord, and I do not know where they have laid him." When she had said this, she turned around and saw Jesus standing there, but she did not know that it was Jesus. Jesus said to her, "Woman, why are you weeping? Whom are you looking for?" Supposing him to be the gardener, she said to him, "Sir, if you have carried him away, tell me where you have laid him, and I will take him away." Jesus said to her, "Mary!" She turned and said to him in Hebrew, "Rabbouni!" (which means Teacher). Jesus said to her, "Do not hold on to me, because I have not yet ascended to the Father. But go to my brothers and say to them, 'I am ascending to my Father and your Father, to my God and your God.'"

—John 20:11–17

Now on that same day two of them were going to a village called Emmaus, about seven miles from Jerusalem, and talking with each other about all these things that had happened. While they were talking and discussing, Jesus himself came near and went with them, but their eyes were kept from recognizing him. And he said to them, "What are you discussing with each other while you walk along?" They stood still, looking sad. Then one of them, whose name was Cleopas, answered him, "Are you the only stranger in Jerusalem who does not know the things that have taken place there in these days?" He asked them, "What things?" They replied, "The things about Jesus of Nazareth, who was a prophet mighty in deed and word before God and all the people, and how our chief priests and leaders handed him over to be condemned to death and crucified him. But we had hoped that he was the one to redeem Israel. Yes, and besides all this, it is now the third day since these things took place. Moreover, some women of our group astounded us. They were at the tomb early this morning, and when they did not find his body there, they came back and told us that they had indeed seen a vision of angels who said that he was alive. Some of those who were with us went to the tomb and found it just as the women had said; but they did not see him." Then he said to them, "Oh, how foolish you are, and how slow of heart to believe all that the prophets have declared! Was it not necessary that the Messiah should suffer these things and then enter into his glory?" Then beginning with Moses and all the prophets, he interpreted to them the things about himself in all the scriptures.

—Luke 24:13–27

Sadness and Loss

Sadness is frequently the dominant feeling we experience in the face of loss—real loss that has taken place or anticipated loss. Most of us experience sadness when a parent dies, even if the relationship has been problematic or broken for some time. I remember coming home from college one weekend and having a quiet breakfast at the kitchen table while my mother was doing some cooking. The phone rang. She answered it, spoke briefly and in a somewhat distant tone. When she hung up she said, "You should go upstairs and talk to your grandmother." My maternal grandmother rented an upstairs apartment behind our garage. It gave her some independence, even as she ate most supper meals with us.

"Yeah, okay," I answered. "I was going to see her later. Was that her on the phone?"

"Yes. The police just came by to tell her that her husband had died, and she's crying."

"Her husband died?" I said, quite shocked. "I thought he'd been dead for decades. Wait a minute," I continued as the fact sunk in. "That's your father! What about you? How do you . . . ?"

"Never mind about me. Go see your grandmother."

Wow! Another major family secret split open without warning. I climbed the stairs slowly, having no idea what I would say or even where to begin. I think I hugged my grandmother when she opened the door and invited me in. She had been crying but told me she wasn't really sad that he died. He'd left her more than twenty-five years earlier. I found out later that he left after numerous business trips with his secretary. Though I knew my grandmother moved from Ohio to California with her two nearly adult daughters, I had been given to believe he had died. I may have been told he left my grandmother. I had suspected alcohol was involved. But no details were given. *And no questions were to be asked.* That was clear.

I talked with my grandmother, mostly listened, actually. She pretty much continued the conspiracy of silence, though she did say she was crying because she didn't have any feelings for him. He had been gone for so long and she had raised her two daughters mostly on her own. After about forty-five minutes, it seemed pretty clear that she was okay and would be uncomfortable if I stayed any longer. I asked if she wanted me to have my mother come up. She said, "No, not unless *she* wants to." I gave her a hug and kiss and left. As I slowly walked down the stairs, I remember hoping that my mother had gone shopping. She hadn't. She wanted to know if Grandma was okay, but when I asked her how she felt knowing that her father had died, she just said, "I didn't really know him, and he left a long, long time ago." End of discussion.

As time went on I was able to gather more details about my grandfather and his role in the life of my mother, her sister, and my grandmother. I have also thought a great deal about the role of secrets in my family and family systems in general. Through sharing stories, teaching, and personal therapy, I am aware of how my own way of dealing with sadness and grief has been affected by my family's choices to avoid discussing their own feelings—for example, anger toward a husband and father who abandons his wife and children; fear of humiliation if people find out the story of deception and cheating; sadness about loss of love and support. The sadness that permeated my family as I grew up was mostly a background odor, like a slightly moldy basement. And there was no permission to speak of what made me sad as a child. After all, not only did we have food that starving orphans went without (we were told this), we also had a father who was faithful to his wife and children. (This, of course, was never explicitly mentioned, lest the secret of Grandpa be unleashed.) All this is to say that sadness was something palpably felt throughout my family of origin, *and* it was never really discussed.

As I have told this story in courses I have taught on pastoral theology and in my consulting and training work, I have found many people who also have deep family secrets. What I have come to understand is that those secrets are not just about the *content* of what is not spoken, they are also about the feelings that were not expressed or sometimes the patterns of substitution (see chapter 8) that arise from the secrets.

As I recall this story, I wonder how my mother's life, and my grandmother's life, and in turn the lives of my father and brother, as well as my life, would have been different if we had all found the room, the permission, the support to experience our sadness, our sorrow, our grief.

I think my wife and I raised children who were not hesitant to express their sadness and talk about what it meant. We all cried at the death of our family pets, even the mice. We spent a day in uncontrollable mourning at the sudden death of a beloved dog fourteen years after we brought her home from the pound. My children do talk about their grandparents, all of whom have been dead for more than eight years. And our family has experienced other losses: moving from the home where my daughters built a tree fort; friends who have moved out of state; career dreams shattered. In these and many other losses, I think we have found the following pattern to hold true.

The schematic of sadness looks like this:

Stimulus →	Feeling →	Message →	Need or Response
Loss (real or anticipated)	**SADNESS**	I am experiencing loss or anticipating loss.	I need to grieve and let go. I may need support, comfort. I liked things as they were.

This general pattern seems to be true for sadness and the message it carries—that I have experienced or am anticipating a real or anticipated loss. However, the need or response each individual has may vary somewhat. Some of us, perhaps the more introverted, suffer our grief more quietly, privately. Others, perhaps in part due to the cultures we inhabit or our ethnic backgrounds, are more demonstrative in our times of loss. We also vary on both the amount of support that we want or what is useful to us and the time it takes to move through our sadness.

The enormous literature on grief, both secular and religious, is much too extensive to rehearse here. Here are a few things I have found useful. My first encounter with grief literature was through

Elisabeth Kübler-Ross, whose classic work *On Death and Dying* introduced the five stages of grieving: denial and isolation, anger, bargaining, depression, and acceptance.[5] Kübler-Ross was careful not to characterize these stages as too linear. Her model allowed for individuals to repeat and recycle through them. Later authors preferred to see the stages more as *tasks* to be accomplished with little regard to the exact order. From the standpoint of feelings, one notes that the process of *grief* is more complicated than the feeling of *sadness* and can include anger and fear.

Melissa M. Kelley, a layperson who teaches at Weston Jesuit School of Theology at Boston College, has written an excellent book, *Grief: Contemporary Theory and the Practice of Ministry.*[6] She articulates the most current psychological thinking on the theory of attachment (including attachment to God), meaning making, and coping. While her psychological and pastoral insights cover the complex process of grieving, they also shed light on how simpler feelings of sadness are related to the losses we experience due to our various attachments. Her work also opens the door to the theological implications of sadness.

Axel Schwaigert has written a wonderful story or guided mediation called "The Village of Grief," in which an individual or group is invited to enter an imaginary village and visit different places in order to engage the dimensions of their grief. The village has a general store where one gets provisions for the journey, a blacksmith shop for hammering out one's anger, a church in which to pray or sit in silence, a pub for connecting with friends in joyful ways and perhaps forgetting one's pain for a while, a library to do reading and research, a hospital for healing and medication. Guides are available to assist the village visitor on their journeys of grief and recovery.[7]

How Sadness Shows Up in the Body

Generally when a person is sad, her heart rate slows and breathing becomes deeper and slower. A sad person may tear up or cry. He may feel listless, a lack of motivation, a lack of appetite. Sad people often complain of finding it difficult to concentrate or make decisions. Sometimes sadness feels like a blow to the stomach or having the bottom fall out of you all at once. The sadness spectrum runs from relatively simple sadness over losing a small amount of money or having a friend cancel a dinner engagement to the grief that comes with the death of one's child or a prolonged depression over losing a job, a home, or a loved one. This chapter focuses primarily on situational and temporary sadness. Malika Ndlovu's poem "Grief" is included above because sometimes a deep grief, even one that has been met and embraced and has found healing, can arise again unexpectedly, causing a new temporary sadness that affects our mood and our relationships. When I feel that sadness, I try to allow myself to experience it for what it is, without passing judgment or telling myself I should be over it.

Deep depression is another matter. According to the *Diagnostic and Statistical Manual of Mental Disorders* (DSM-IV), the emotional symptoms of depression include constant sadness, irritability, hopelessness, feeling worthless or guilty for no reason, and loss of interest in favorite activities.[8] Physical symptoms of depression include trouble sleeping, low energy or fatigue, significant weight change, and difficulty concentrating. Those experiencing any of the symptoms of depression should check with their primary care physician, a counselor, or clergyperson. Depression is treatable and need not be suffered in isolation.

Sadness and Connection

If Melissa Kelley is right, and I think she is, sadness has to do with attachments. We are sad when we suffer the loss of someone or something to which we have formed a significant connection or attachment. Sadness might be the result of a break in connection. In discussing anger, I mentioned that anger can arise when I feel that another has broken connection with me or when I encounter an obstacle to a deeper connection that I long for. In these cases, I often hold the other person partly responsible for the quality of the connection. My anger may also tell me that I would like to renegotiate the terms of the relationship. Sadness more often arises when that connection is lost, perhaps through death or distance, without any attribution of wrongdoing and with little or less hope of renegotiation. The break in connection, the loss, is what I experience with little attention to the reason behind it. I enjoyed the connection, and now it is gone and I am sad. I have a friend who expected to be in her dear friend's wedding as a bridesmaid. She received a "Save the Date" note for the wedding date and found the list of the wedding party on a social media site. She was angry. She made numerous attempts to contact her so-called friend to investigate or renegotiate the relationship—to no avail. After some months the anger passed. Sadness about the loss remained.

Sadness can also be the opening for greater connection with others around me who respond to my sadness by accompanying me or comforting me. Though I may feel both anger and sadness about a loss or a break in connection, sadness is more likely to invite others to walk alongside me. Though I might seek allies in pursuit of justice when I am righteously angry, most of us have been more socially conditioned to accompany another person in their sadness more easily than in their anger.

Ira Byock, a leading palliative care physician, talks about four phrases that carry enormous power for a dying person: "Please forgive me," "I forgive you," "Thank you," and "I love you."[9] They are phrases that express connection and are particularly poignant for a person who is dying and for those who love him. I have found these same phrases are important when clergy or lay staff members leave a congregation, or when leaders make the transition off a congregational board. They are ways of both acknowledging a connection and marking a transition. They are ways of marking the impending loss.

Sadness and Gender

As was the case with anger, those of us who identify as female and those of us who identify as male have been socially conditioned differently with regard to the permission we have to experience and to express our sadness. Generally speaking, in similar situations, women are given more freedom to be sad than men. A woman's "extended" sadness may be tolerated, while men are much more likely to be told to "buck up" or "get over it." Under similar conditions, women may be referred to as sensitive, while men may be called "soft" or even "effeminate." In February 1972, former governor and then senator from Maine Edmund Muskie was a leading contender for the Democratic nomination for president. At one time, polls said that he would have beaten Richard Nixon had the election been undertaken early. In response to personal attacks on his wife, Muskie gave an emotional speech. The press reported he cried, though he later said the "tears" were melting snowflakes due to the weather outside. Though there were other factors that led to his failure to be the Democratic nominee in 1972, many political analysts of the time attributed his decline in the polls to his emotional speech, which shattered his image as a calm and reasoned leader.

Though it has certainly become more permissible for men to cry or to show other signs of sadness publically, it is still true that sadness in men can easily be portrayed as a lack of so-called manhood and thus an inability to lead. I am reminded of my wife and another friend who have said, "I can cry [be sad] and still think!"

Congregational Sadness

Some congregations that have suffered disproportional losses of mostly male leaders and members due to the HIV/AIDS epidemic in the 1980s have displayed a corporate sadness that few other churches have experienced in a similar way. The loss for the relatively young Metropolitan Community Church (MCC) of nearly one thousand key leaders was devastating because of the talent and potential for ministry and growth that was lost and unrealized. Both on the congregational level and the denominational level, the emotional soul of the faithful community was tested. Individual funerals did all they could to speak to the deep personal sadness of family and friends. Political funerals, such as that of Steve Michael, founder of ACT UP Washington DC, on June 4, 1998, drew attention to the travesty of low financial support for health research, HIV prevention, and subsidized health care. Yet even these public-protest funerals were unable to lessen the growing numbness that the HIV/AIDS community and its allies were feeling over the enormous contagion of sadness that the community felt. This sadness, to a large extent unaddressed, complicated the emergence of women as clergy within the MCC denomination. While women's struggles for recognition in church leadership has been fairly universal, the corporate sadness and allied feelings of survivor guilt in this denomination complicated the rise of women to positions of leadership locally and nationally.[10]

Congregations that have experienced the death of key leaders in close succession or even a single leader due to tragic circumstances often exhibit a corporate sadness for an extended period. I once served a church in which two retired church secretaries who had served consecutively for more than forty years died within a month of one another. After the deaths, the "new" secretary of nearly two and a half years began reporting that she was having much more difficulty obtaining the normal information and reports for the church bulletin and newsletter. People who normally showed up for committee meetings and liturgical responsibilities were more often late or absent. Though the funerals and lengthy testimonials at the receptions following the funerals and celebration of these women had seemed appropriate and robust, a couple of months passed before corporate life returned to normal. It was as though the death of these former key officeholders meant that the business they had overseen in their day could not proceed, even though the current secretary was far more skilled technically and was a very warm individual with exceptional relational skills. She knew what was happening but was powerless to do anything about the efficiency slide. Had I been more affectively competent at the time, I might have engaged the church board as well as other key groups (the choir, the lay liturgical leaders, the Sunday school teachers) in an open discussion of their sadness and its impact on the congregation as a whole.

On a more positive note, many Christian congregations invite members to purchase Christmas and Easter flowers as an opportunity to remember their loved ones. In some Christian traditions, the Feast of All Saints (November 1) or All Souls (November 2) is another time for personal memorials. Some congregations also have on-site cemeteries, columbaria, memorial gardens, or plaques that function not simply to remember individuals but also to say that our spiritual forebears are still an important part of this community. One might ask how these occasions might better express the corporate loss, grief, and celebration of the people of the congregation. In a similar way, a "rogues gallery" of former pastors reminds people of the ordained leadership history in the congregation. Such a gallery often gives a double-edged message, however, since it is usually dominated by men and emphasizes clergy leadership without holding up images of lay leaders.

Resources

Byock, Ira. *The Four Things that Matter Most: A Book about Living.* New York: Free Press, 2004. A palliative care physician talks about four phrases that carry enormous power for a dying person and those closest to that person: "Please forgive me," "I forgive you," "Thank you," and "I love you."

Hamman, Jaco J. *When Steeples Cry: Leading Congregations through Loss and Change.* Cleveland, OH: Pilgrim Press, 2005. The author suggests ways congregational leaders can facilitate the grieving process through conversations, public worship, and ministries of compassion.

McFayden, Kenneth J. *Strategic Leadership for a Change: Facing Our Losses, Finding Our Future.* Herndon, VA: Alban Institute, 2009. While taking the pain of loss seriously, the author articulates how vision can promote change by attending to stories and values.

Oswald, Roy. *Running through the Thistles.* Herndon, VA: Alban Institute, 1978. Alban author and congregational consultant Oswald argues that the way a pastor leaves a congregation either supports or undermines most of the ministry he or she did as pastor. Attention must be paid to self, others, and programs when leaving.

Schaper, Donna. *Mature Grief: When a Parent Dies.* Cambridge, MA: Cowley Publications, 2002. Pastorally wise advice for the loss nearly all people face.

Reflection Questions

Personal Level

1. How did your parents and other significant people in your life as you were growing up express sadness?
2. When you were sad as a child, were you able to express your sadness? How did you express it? How did others around you respond?
3. What personal losses have you experienced recently? The loss of a beloved family member, relative, friend? A close colleague or neighbor? A job? A favorite pet?
4. Who has moved away from you recently? Literally? Figuratively?
5. Do any of these losses bring back into consciousness a significant loss from your childhood?
6. What do you most need at a time of loss? To be alone? To be with someone who understands and comforts? To be in quiet prayer?

Congregational Level

1. Has your congregation experienced significant loss recently? Retired pastor or rabbi, secretary, organist or music director, education coordinator? Has the congregation experienced a substantial loss of membership or income? What has been the impact of these losses on the community?
2. What losses are not being talked about? What grief is not being expressed here? How might the loss and grief become subjects of discussion?
3. Does the congregation or the elected leadership have a process to terminate programs, or do programs merely

fade away when no one assumes the next round of leadership? For example, how might the secondhand clothing store or the women's auxiliary receive an appropriate and celebratory funeral instead of simply disappearing, without comment, from the annual report?

4. How do people exit the congregation? In what ways are the presence and contributions of members acknowledged when they move away?

Chapter 5

Peace

Peace I leave with you; my peace I give you. I do not give to you as the world gives. Do not let your hearts be troubled, and do not let them be afraid.

—John 14:27

As you read the poetry and scripture in this chapter, I invite you to be aware of your own peace—at knowing that you are loved and precious, that the Holy One knew you before you were in your mother's womb, that nothing can separate you from the love of God.

Recall a time when you felt completely calm and in tune with yourself and the world you inhabit. Allow yourself to reexperience the peacefulness. (Perhaps on the seashore or on a mountain peak. Perhaps in a lovely chapel or cathedral.) Where were you? Were you alone or were others with you? What were you seeing, hearing, smelling?

Stay as long as you wish in this place of peace.

Stop reading at any point to write in a journal or to call a companion to read a passage aloud. Recall your own favorite poems, stories, works of art, and Scripture passages that relate to joy.

As a free writing exercise, write for five minutes beginning with one of the following prompts:

I am peaceful when . . .
or
Peace is . . .

On a beautiful morning you walk in the woods.
You are alone with the woods, the light and the shadow,
   the shades of green leaves freshly bathed with rain, sun rays
   dancing on the branches through the leaves on the ground.
You did not go there to acquire something.
You went there to be with the trees, with other beings.
To be, not to obtain, not to acquire.
     —*Vimala Thakar, The Eloquence of Living*[1]

Deep peace I breathe into you, O weariness, here:
O ache, here!
Deep peace, a soft white dove to you;
Deep peace, a quiet rain to you;
Deep peace, an ebbing wave to you!
Deep peace, red wind of the east from you;
Deep peace, grey wind of the west to you;
Deep peace, dark wind of the north from you;

Deep peace, blue wind of the south to you!
Deep peace, pure red of the flame to you;
Deep peace, pure white of the moon to you;
Deep peace, pure green of the grass to you;
Deep peace, pure brown of the earth to you;
Deep peace, pure grey of the dew to you,
Deep peace, pure blue of the sky to you!
Deep peace of the running wave to you,
Deep peace of the flowing air to you,
Deep peace of the quiet earth to you,
Deep peace of the sleeping stones to you!
Deep peace of the Yellow Shepherd to you,
Deep peace of the Wandering Shepherdess to you,
Deep peace of the Flock of Stars to you,
Deep peace from the Son of Peace to you,
Deep peace from the heart of Mary to you,
And from Briget of the Mantle
Deep peace, deep peace!
And with the kindness too of the Haughty Father
Peace!
In the name of the Three who are One,
Peace!
And by the will of the King of the Elements,
Peace! Peace!

—*Fiona Macleod, "Amadan"*[2]

⌣

The Year's at the Spring
The year's at the spring,
And day's at the morn;
Morning's at seven;
The hill-side's dew-pearled;
The lark's on the wing;
The snail's on the thorn;
God's in his Heaven—
All's right with the world!

—*Robert Browning*[3]

⌣

Fern Hill
Now as I was young and easy under the apple boughs
About the lilting house and happy as the grass was green,

The night above the dingle starry,
Time let me hail and climb
Golden in the heydays of his eyes,
And honoured among wagons I was prince of the apple towns
And once below a time I lordly had the trees and leaves
Trail with daisies and barley
Down the rivers of the windfall light.
And as I was green and carefree, famous among the barns
About the happy yard and singing as the farm was home,
In the sun that is young once only,
Time let me play and be
Golden in the mercy of his means,
And green and golden I was huntsman and herdsman, the calves
Sang to my horn, the foxes on the hills barked clear and cold,
And the sabbath rang slowly
In the pebbles of the holy streams.
All the sun long it was running, it was lovely, the hay
Fields high as the house, the tunes from the chimneys, it was air
And playing, lovely and watery
And fire green as grass.
And nightly under the simple stars
As I rode to sleep the owls were bearing the farm away,
All the moon long I heard, blessed among stables, the nightjars
Flying with the ricks, and the horses
Flashing into the dark.
And then to awake, and the farm, like a wanderer white
With the dew, come back, the cock on his shoulder: it was all
Shining, it was Adam and maiden,
The sky gathered again
And the sun grew round that very day.
So it must have been after the birth of the simple light
In the first, spinning place, the spellbound horses walking warm
Out of the whinnying green stable
On to the fields of praise.
And honoured among foxes and pheasants by the gay house
Under the new made clouds and happy as the heart was long,
In the sun born over and over,
I ran my heedless ways,
My wishes raced through the house high hay
And nothing I cared, at my sky blue trades, that time allows
In all his tuneful turning so few and such morning songs
Before the children green and golden
Follow him out of grace.

Nothing I cared, in the lamb white days, that time would take me
Up to the swallow thronged loft by the shadow of my hand,
In the moon that is always rising,
Nor that riding to sleep
I should hear him fly with the high fields
And wake to the farm forever fled from the childless land.
Oh as I was young and easy in the mercy of his means,
Time held me green and dying
Though I sang in my chains like the sea.

—Dylan Thomas[4]

Growth into the freedom of peace and silence is not the privilege
   of a chosen few.
It is the natural state of being for everyone.
We don't have to create freedom; it is there as the substance of
   reality.
We only have to let the false drop noiselessly.

—Vimala Thakar, The Eloquence of Living[5]

They shall beat their swords into plowshares,
and their spears into pruning-hooks;
nation shall not lift up sword against nation,
neither shall they learn war any more.

—Isaiah 2:4b

The wolf shall live with the lamb,
the leopard shall lie down with the kid,
the calf and the lion and the fatling together,
and a little child shall lead them.
The cow and the bear shall graze,
their young shall lie down together;
and the lion shall eat straw like the ox.
The nursing child shall play over the hole of the asp,
and the weaned child shall put its hand on the adder's den.
They will not hurt or destroy
on all my holy mountain;
for the earth will be full of the knowledge of the Lord
as the waters cover the sea.

—Isaiah 11:6–9

If I ascend to heaven, you are there;
if I make my bed in Sheol, you are there.
If I take the wings of the morning
and settle at the farthest limits of the sea,
even there your hand shall lead me,
and your right hand shall hold me fast.
If I say, "Surely the darkness shall cover me,
and the light around me become night,"
even the darkness is not dark to you;
the night is as bright as the day,
for darkness is as light to you.
For it was you who formed my inward parts;
you knit me together in my mother's womb.
I praise you, for I am fearfully and wonderfully made.
Wonderful are your works;
that I know very well.
My frame was not hidden from you,
when I was being made in secret,
intricately woven in the depths of the earth.
Your eyes beheld my unformed substance.
In your book were written
all the days that were formed for me,
when none of them as yet existed.

> —*Psalm 139:8–16*

Trust in the LORD and do good;
so you will live in the land, and enjoy security.
Take delight in the LORD,
and he will give you the desires of your heart.
Commit your way to the LORD;
trust in him, and he will act.
He will make your vindication shine like the light,
and the justice of your cause like the noonday.
Be still before the LORD, and wait patiently for him;
do not fret over those who prosper in their way,
over those who carry out evil devices.

> —*Psalm 37:3–7*

God is in the midst of the city; it shall not be moved;
God will help it when the morning dawns.

The nations are in an uproar, the kingdoms totter;
he utters his voice, the earth melts.
The LORD of hosts is with us;
the God of Jacob is our refuge.
Come, behold the works of the LORD;
see what desolations he has brought on the earth.
He makes wars cease to the end of the earth;
he breaks the bow, and shatters the spear;
he burns the shields with fire.
"Be still, and know that I am God!
I am exalted among the nations,
I am exalted in the earth."
The LORD of hosts is with us;
the God of Jacob is our refuge.
                                    —*Psalm 46:5–11*

While they were talking about this, Jesus himself stood among them and said to them, "Peace be with you." They were startled and terrified, and thought that they were seeing a ghost. He said to them, "Why are you frightened, and why do doubts arise in your hearts? Look at my hands and my feet; see that it is I myself. Touch me and see; for a ghost does not have flesh and bones as you see that I have." And when he had said this, he showed them his hands and his feet. While in their joy they were disbelieving and still wondering, he said to them, "Have you anything here to eat?" They gave him a piece of broiled fish, and he took it and ate in their presence.
                                    —*Luke 24:36–43*

Cultivating Peace

For more than twenty years, my spouse and I have met with another couple one evening a month to meditate for thirty minutes and then have supper. After we meditate, we often spend a few minutes talking about the experience and how our spiritual practice has been going during the past month. Over dinner, usually take-out Chinese food, we talk about our children, what we have been reading or writing, politics, and—as we have aged—our state of health. Our friends are culturally Jewish and spiritually Buddhist. In that and many other ways, we are quite different from one another. Yet in more than twenty years of meditating silently with one another, as a monthly discipline, we have developed a rhythm that allows us to easily slip into a peaceful space with ourselves and with one another. I imagine that it helps that we are nearly always in the same space, a room devoted to mediation in their house, and that we meet at about the same time each month. It is also helpful to me that our time of meditation begins and ends with the striking of a singing bowl that calls us into a sacred time and space and later brings us back into one another's presence. I think it also helps that we each have our own practice of meditating, though for me our monthly meetings are the most regular and long-lived of my current spiritual practices.

Over the years, there have been many occasions when most of my meditation has been spent chasing distractions or being chased by them—even though I *know* to let them drift away. Occasionally, the thirty minutes will pass in a flash. Sometimes, I actually fall asleep. Not to worry, I tell myself. I think it was Teresa of Avila who said that sleep is very close to prayer. But nearly every time I meditate, there is at least a small window in which I feel deeply relaxed, at peace, connected to myself, to those who may be in the room, to others I love who may be thousands of miles away or even no longer alive. I treasure those moments of deep peace.

I begin with this story because it seems to me that being *peaceful* is something that requires cultivation for me. As with all feelings, being peaceful can arise naturally, as a response to a stimulus. Listening to certain music, usually soft classical music or cool jazz, works for me. Tony Scott's *Music for Zen Meditation* and Dave Brubeck's *Brandenburg Gate Revisited* are particular favorites of mine.[6] Lying on a quiet beach or walking in the woods or sitting on a mountain peak can also stimulate a sense of peacefulness for me. Visiting a beautiful cathedral or a quiet country chapel can bring great peace. Sitting for five minutes in the office of my dear friend and colleague, Katherine, settles me into relationship with my core being about as quickly as anything. I believe all these responses are just that—responses to various stimuli that evoke a calm connectedness to my core being, to the Divine within me, and to all creation. Yet because I am surrounded by so much noise most of time, I often miss what could be opportunities for feeling or being peaceful.

To speak about cultivating peacefulness may sound contradictory to the whole idea that feelings are a response. As the son and grandson of farmers, and having spent two summers working on the farm where my father grew up, I appreciate the intentionality of cultivating crops. When I worked on the farm, for example, before the corn was planted, the ground was tilled. The hard ground was broken up so that some of the moister soil came to the surface and the weeds were turned under. After the corn was planted, it was twice cultivated, meaning someone carefully drove a tractor between the rows while tiny hoes loosened the soil to each side of the freshly sprouting corn and again turned under some weeds. The corn *itself* responded to the stimulus of the minerals and nutrients in the soil, to the sun, and to the rain. *And* the process of natural growth was augmented by the intentionality of breaking up the soil and removing as much as possible the weeds that were competing for the nutrients. In a similar way, I think I benefit from intentionally trying to notice the weeds that are competing for time and energy in my everyday environment.

While other emotions may arise for me with a blunt directness, peace comes at me more subtly, and I can easily dismiss it as a distraction. I think my childhood set me up for not noticing peacefulness. My mother was an omnipresent and fairly anxious person. I remember being asked to draw a picture of the house I lived in as a child and placing all my family members in various rooms. I drew my mother in every room of the house. My father was in his workshop in the garage. I was in a storage room behind the garage that I had turned into a bedroom in an attempt to have more personal space and peace. As I look back on my growing years, it seems the peace I experienced was mostly what I intentionally created for myself, and it was often a sense of not being hassled or smothered by my mother. So I am still working on believing that peace can arise spontaneously in response to a stimulus. I am still learning to set aside my hypervigilance so that I can notice and respond to a beautiful sunset or to the calm of sitting in silence in Katherine's office.

You may wish to draw a scene from your early childhood, placing members of your family in the house where you grew up. Note where you found the most peace at home or some special place to which you turned.

Sabbath

The practice of shabbat or sabbath has a long history in Jewish, Muslim, and Christian traditions, whether it is kept on Saturday, Friday, or Sunday. Since the time of Gautama Buddha (500 BCE), many Buddhists have also observed Uposatha, every seven or eight days (following a lunar calendar), as a time for the cleansing of the defiled mind, with the intended result of inner calm. These community ritual observations are meant to open space for individuals to nurture inward peace. My experience has been that individuals and congregations who are faithful to sabbath time radiate a calm that is countercultural. They are going against the anxious tide of worldly cares as communities of faith in much the same way I felt I was struggling to fit quiet space in my household growing up. Putting myself in the presence of sabbath-observant individuals and congregations on a regular basis has been life changing.

On a cultural level, we all live in a global household that is anxious, frenzied, demanding. The hustle and bustle of the world may seem to take up occupancy in every room of our being. Staving off that invasion is nearly impossible work for an individual, unless you are inclined to live in a yurt in the desert. Communities that practice sabbath, that stand against the tide of producing and consuming 24/7, offer an alternative. They offer the opportunity to look at the hectic patterns we imbibe and inscribe. But even more than holding up a mirror to how we rush or flee through the week, they offer a timeout, a respite, and even the possibility of experiencing peace. Such communities become holding environments, sanctuaries that make a peaceful response to inner and outer stimuli possible.

Feeling grateful is akin to feeling peaceful. When I am grateful, I feel a sense of inner harmony along with a connection to another person or the Divine. Eucharist, as a thanksgiving meal, is meant to cultivate the feeling of peace. Many an early morning Eucharist with sparse attendance and no music has touched my being deeply and given me strength for the day or week ahead. It would be a shame if, in our attempts to enliven contemporary worship to make it more appealing, we lost the peace-engendering possibilities that are indigenous to a simple Eucharist. When I was a campus minister in the South in the 1970s, the Sunday night candlelight Eucharist was well attended by students of many religious backgrounds, some of whom came back from weekends at home in time to renew their spirits before another week of study. The service was simple, the music soft, the sermon reflective. The widespread popularity of Celtic worship speaks to this same desire of many people for simplicity that fosters inner peace. For others, yoga, sitting or walking meditation, and the use of the labyrinth offer ways to cultivate peace.

The pattern that generates peacefulness and its message and response looks like this:

Stimulus →	Feeling →	Message →	Need or Response
Serene setting;	**PEACEFUL**	I am centered.	Continue to be
deep awareness		I am connected.	focused.
of connection		Maintain connection	
		to God and myself	
		(and others).	

The *peaceful* feeling family includes content, intimate, trusting, relaxed, serene, thankful, and loving. Peaceful is a more inward feeling than joyful; the energy is calmer. The stimulus for feeling peaceful can be either a serene setting (lying in a hammock hearing the breeze in the trees) or a deep awareness of being connected. I feel peaceful when I have written a difficult letter and know that I have spoken honestly about what needed to be said in order for me to reconnect with someone with integrity. I feel peaceful when I am in right relationship with those who are important to me. When I feel peaceful, the message is "I am centered." My need is for things to stay as they are. I want to prolong the inner calm state I am in, even if, and perhaps especially if, I must soon move back into my normal, busier life.

How Peacefulness Shows Up in the Body

When I am peaceful, my heart rate usually slows down. My breathing is deeper, slower, and more regular. In fact, with practice, I can become more peaceful by intentionally breathing deeper and more slowly. When I am peaceful, the colors around me seem brighter. My vision is clearer. Life has a more vivid 3-D quality without being overwhelming. My movements are a bit slower, less random, more intentional and efficient. Ironically, when I am most at peace, I may be extremely attentive to my surroundings (people, environment, sounds, textures, breezes), or I may have tuned out most of what is exterior to me. When I am most centered, for example when meditating, I might even be without inner mental and physical distractions, if only for brief moments.

Peace and Connection

As I think about feeling peaceful, the connections that arise most immediately are with myself, with nature, and with God. I think this comes from my need to be peaceful with myself, to be connected to my voice, my being, before I can connect with others. The exception, of course, is connecting with someone who exudes peace, or at least presents a calm, peaceful presence when I encounter her. I have a few treasured friends like that. When I feel peace deprived, I head their way. Sometimes even making a date to see them puts me in a more serene mood. And when I am with such a person, the serenity seems to amplify. It is as though we each become more tuned in to our centered state. Before digital radio tuning, I remember fidgeting with the radio dial to get the clearest signal. The farther away you were from the broadcast station, for instance when traveling, the harder it was to find the frequency that would receive the radio signal. I remember visiting someone with a really good radio that had a large tuning knob that made getting on the right wavelength much easier. Being with a peaceful friend is like having the broadcast station closer or having the signal amplified. It's easier for both of us to tune in, to be centered. When this person shares core beliefs and values about the Source of Peace and the ultimate worth of each of us as created in the divine image, the peaceful tuning may be even deeper and clearer.

Not everyone I meet exudes serenity, and even the most centered of my friends can have their frantic days. At those times it may be up to me to carry the peaceful tune. At times I have experienced myself being quite calm, even peaceful, in the presence of someone who is very angry, scared, or sad, but this usually takes a great deal of focus on my part. The peace I feel in such circumstances is not a response to an external stimulus but rather a secondary peace that I achieve or that is achieved within me. It is almost in spite of the stimuli around me.

Being peaceful is sometimes a pathway to connecting with another person. When I *am* peaceful in a tense setting or with an unfamiliar person, I am drawing upon an inner strength. I am showing up in a centered, calm way. I am allowing myself to be vulnerable, open, and responsive, because I am not in a state of anxiety. I am comfortable in my own skin. If someone wishes me harm or is set on being antagonistic toward me, that person may find my peacefulness irritating and deem it to be cause for further provocation. In such cases it is hard to remain peaceful. In such settings, I find myself praying for the other person or envisioning him or her as surrounded by light and healing. My hope is that the peace I feel will rub off on the other person or form a bridge between me and the other. Obviously, we cannot force peace on another person. Peace, in the sense of the inner feeling of harmony or centeredness, cannot be coerced. At the same time, being truly peaceful within oneself may ultimately be the *only* way to begin to make connection when there has been serious disconnection or a history of broken relationships.

A couple of years after I was ordained, I worked part time in a day-treatment program of a county mental health center in South Carolina. The adult clients were people who were transitioning from a residential, locked mental health facility and other people who were judged to need significant ongoing care for seven to eight hours a day but who had not chosen or were not consigned to a residential program. Each day began with forty-five minutes of gentle yoga. Attention was placed on stretching, becoming as limber as one's body would allow, and breathing deeply and slowly. Most of the focus was on breathing. Often clients were not sure what this had to do with their treatment, but most cooperated to some extent. While the instructors (members of the therapy team) talked people through the exercises, there were also significant periods of silence or sitting with gentle music playing.

At first I too questioned the utility of these forty-five minutes of "wasted time." Over time I came to realize how beginning with that peaceful time was significant for people who were beset with voices constantly gnawing at them or with enormous questions of self-worth. This was a sabbath, a timeout in which individuals could connect to what was good within them, to a "higher power" or "spirit of life," if they so chose. They also connected to the other clients and the staff who were all doing the same exercises and breathing. No hierarchies of knowledge, wellness, insights, or power were present. The slow, deep breathing also established a pattern to which clients could return when they became anxious, sad, or angry. Sometimes a hand gently placed on a client's back or the suggestion "Return to your deep breathing" was all it took to invite a person to return to an emotional state that allowed him to notice his feelings and experience them without being completely overwhelmed or at the mercy of what he was experiencing.

Peace and Gender

Whether we speak of peace as a feeling in response to a stimulus or peace in the more political sense (see below), peace seems to mean something different to women and to men.[7] As I listen to women talk about being peaceful or feeling peaceful, my sense is that they are describing a process or a relational way of being. Peaceful can describe both *how* people interact and the feeling that women (sometimes men) have in response to experiencing others engaged in meaningful, healing interactions. As I listen to men talk, feeling peaceful or being peaceful is more about an outcome or end product.[8] I think men more often feel peaceful when they have achieved something, such as closing a tense deal or landing a new job. Even being on vacation, when it is described as peaceful, is about having arrived at a destination. To the extent that men and women are referring to different stimuli or contexts for feeling peaceful, the messages about maintaining one's centeredness or being connected with others have different nuances. For women, feeling peaceful may mean staying with the process; for men feeling peaceful may mean ensuring that they attain a desired outcome and that the outcome does not change.

While I have focused on these differences as they relate to gender, one might also investigate the differences as they correlate to Myers-Briggs personality types. Thus those who incline toward being judging (J) would experience peace more as a product and those inclined to being perceiving (P) would experience peace more as a process.[9]

The Cherokee poet and essayist Marilou Awaikta tells a powerful story about how her people view gender, power, and peace.

> "Where are your women?"
>
> The speaker is Attakullakulla, a Cherokee chief renowned for his shrewd and effective diplomacy. He has come to negotiate a treaty with the whites. Among his delegation are women "as famous in war, as powerful in the council." Their presence also has ceremonial significance: it is meant to show honor to the other delegation. But that delegation is composed of males only; to them the absence of women is irrelevant, a trivial consideration.
>
> To the Cherokee, however, reverence for women/Mother Earth/life/spirit is interconnected. Irreverence for one is likely to mean irreverence for all. Implicit in their chief's question, "Where are your women?" the Cherokee hear, "Where is your balance? What is your intent?" They see that balance is absent and are wary of white men's motives. They intuit the mentality of destruction.[10]

This story points to cultural differences between "whites" and Native peoples. I relate the story because it illustrates the belief that the presence and active participation of women will result in a different outcome regarding peace, *and* that feelings about what is safe or peaceful are connected to the presence of the feminine. This story also serves as a transition to talking about peace as a political reality or goal.

Political Peace (Peace and Power)

Unlike the other emotions, peace has a significant political meaning. Countries are said to be *at peace* or at war with one another. Peace can describe a state of nonconflict between individuals, groups, communities, or nations. The term *peace* is used here to identify an outcome, the lack of conflict or hostility. This is different from the use of the word for the feeling one experiences in response to a stimulus. Because politics is all about power—both power over and power with—it is important to pay attention to how power is being used or abused when talking about *achieving peace* between parties in conflict. When power is used to oppress or force another into compliance or submission, peace is not achieved. Conformity, order, resolution of the conflict may be attained, but the basic inequality of power will likely mean that the resolution will only last as long as the imbalance of power is maintained. Peace is more about empowerment or working to ensure that power is shared.

As I think about peace and power, I am reminded of a comment my daughter Susannah made when she was about ten years old. I was preparing to preach on Ephesians 6:10–20, Paul's analogy of putting on "the whole armor of God." The irony of the passage is that many early followers of Jesus refused to take up a sword or a shield when condemned to fight gladiators in an arena. They believed their executioners were their brothers, so they would not fight. Nor would they join the army. So Paul's exhortation to put on the armor of God must have been shocking. After discussing what I would say about the sword of truth and the breastplate of righteousness, I said I was puzzled about why Paul would urge his readers, "As shoes for your feet put on whatever will make you ready to proclaim the gospel of peace." Why associate peace with feet? Why not arms to embrace others or ears to listen? Was it just because military equipment in Paul's day included some sort of foot protection? Susannah said, "It's simple, Dad. If you are going to make peace, you have to be able to move." Peace is not static. You have to be able to move toward others in mutual relationship.

Peaceful Communities

I suspect that most people's first associations with peaceful communities are monasteries or convents, the Society of Friends (Quakers), or a Buddhist community. Associating peace with monasteries and convents likely derives from the distance that professed religious men and women (both Christian and Buddhist) create between themselves and the hustle and bustle of the world beyond them or the amount of time they spend in silence and prayer. Anyone who has lived in or come to know such groups of people can attest to the normal human strife that is part of even the best monastery or convent. Our association of Quakers with peaceful communities comes from their practice of silence and their intention to live in harmony with one another. What would it mean if churches and synagogues incorporated more silence into their services and board or congregational meetings? How would committing to being more *intentionally* peaceful change the behaviors and practices of faith communities?

The absence of words, music, noise, or social media does not in itself lead to individual or communal peacefulness. Silence does not ensure listening. Being centered, focused, and connected as a community requires habitual attention and lots of practice. Buddhists even speak of their meditation and the way of life that flows from it as their "practice." I have noticed that congregations that incorporate silence into their worship services are more likely to *practice* listening in their educational programs, board and committee meetings, and annual meetings. The blessing that silence receives in worship can transfer into more secular dimensions of life. The practice of being silent after Scripture readings, a sermon, and shared Communion allows church members to attune to God's presence among them and within them so that at other times tuning to that same channel is easier. In the consulting work I do, I often interrupt an animated exchange to ask for a few moments of silence. Then I ask a question such as "What did you hear people saying?" or "What was just going on?" These questions get at the *process* of peace that I spoke about in the gender section above. The pause and questions also address imbalances of power. Interrupting a rapidly flowing interaction allows more introverted people a chance to get into the discussion and invites more extroverted people to pause and notice their behaviors.

The other intervention I often make after a pause for silence is to invite the group to notice what they are feeling. This tactic works best if people have had a chance to learn how feelings carry messages and what those messages are. The societal default, especially at meetings, is to favor thinking or doing. Making room for the expression of feelings and for reflection upon what the feelings are telling us changes the culture. Attending to feelings and their meanings is part of becoming a more peaceful community, because peace is about being *internally connected*, about allowing our thoughts, beliefs, behaviors, and feelings to speak to one another and be heard by one another.

C. Otto Scharmer, who teaches at both the MIT Sloan School of Management and the Helsinki School of Economics, talks about *presencing* as the transition period from the *letting go* of old ways of thinking and acting to the *letting come* of creative new ways of thinking, being, and doing.[11] Presencing often involves a profound silence that has a deeply peaceful quality. Authors who write about transformation and change most frequently stress feelings of fear, anger, and sadness and discuss the resistance of communities to change. Scharmer's *Theory U* also speaks of these feelings, especially fear.[12] What is remarkable is the emphasis he and his colleagues place on practices of meditation and particularly their discovery that many significant changes in corporations and societal movements include a period of communal silence and peace. In the words of Joseph Jaworski, cofounder of the Global

Leadership Initiative and coauthor with Scharmer, presencing is a critical step as a group or civic community moves from their awareness of a limited field of possibilities to "a larger, underlying field that goes beyond what exists now and opens up this great power and beauty."[13]

The Quakers have developed a corporate practice called a *clearness committee.* A person who is trying to discern a vocation or struggling with an issue gathers four or five people who will ask them open and honest questions that may assist them in making a decision. The process includes a lot of silence, and advice giving is prohibited. Toward the end of the process, the committee may mirror back what they observed in the discerner. For example, "When you spoke about x, your voice dropped and your energy was flat; when you spoke about y, your energy rose and you leaned forward in your chair." Clearness committees and similar processes are both more peaceful in their methodology and generally lead to the discerner feeling connected, centered, and peaceful at their conclusion.[14]

Resources

Hanh, Thich Nhat. *Peace Is Every Step: The Path of Mindfulness in Everyday Life.* Edited by Arnold Kotler. New York: Bantam, 1992. Hanh, a Vietnamese monk, a renowned Zen master, a poet, and a peace activist, shows us how to make positive use of the very situations that usually pressure and antagonize us. For him a ringing telephone can be a signal to call us back to our true selves. Dirty dishes, red lights, and traffic jams are spiritual friends on the path to mindfulness—the process of keeping our consciousness alive to our present experience and reality. The most profound satisfactions, the deepest feelings of joy and completeness lie as close at hand as our next aware breath.

Leadingham, Carrie, Joann E. Moschella, and Hilary M. Vartanian, eds. *Peace Prayers: Meditations, Affirmations, Invocations, Poems, and Prayers for Peace.* San Francisco: HarperSanFrancisco, 1991. Originally conceived as a response to the Gulf War, this book is a compilation of prayers, meditations, affirmations, poems, quotations, and reflections on peace from a variety of perspectives. In addition to original contributions from popular authors, this book contains selections from the works of figures such as Maya Angelou, Rabbi Harold Kushner, Vaclav Havel, Albert Einstein, and Martin Luther King, Jr..

Roberts, Elizabeth, and Elias Amidon, eds. *Earth Prayers from Around the World: 365 Prayers, Poems, and Invocations for Honoring the Earth.* San Francisco: HarperSanFrancisco, 1991. Selections from Hildegard of Bingen, Thich Nhat Hanh, Black Elk, the Rig Veda, Margaret Atwood, and Hebrew and Christian Scriptures.

Senge, Peter, C. Otto Scharmer, Joseph Jaworski, and Betty Sue Flowers. *Presence: An Exploration of Profound Change in People, Organization, and Society.* New York: Doubleday, 2004. These internationally renowned consultants and trainers value the intellectual and emotional dimensions of change as well as write about taking risks in prototyping new ways of acting corporately and communally. They work with people to create innovative health care systems, sustainable agriculture, and less corporate waste. Individual and corporate spiritual practices play a significant role in many of their stories.

Reflection Questions

Personal Level

1. How comfortable are you with silence?
2. When was the last time you took a real sabbath day to nurture your soul, to connect with the Divine within you in a deeply nourishing way? What would you have to change in order to take sabbaths more often?
3. What practices give rise to peacefulness in you? Journal writing, listening to quiet music, prayer or meditation, walking a labyrinth, gardening, woodworking, making bread, visiting an art gallery, working out at the gym?

4. Who are the peaceful people in your life? Do you have allies for nurturing peace within yourself and in your relationships?

Congregational Level

1. Are there periods of silence in your congregation's corporate worship? If so, how do you respond to them? If not, how could they be added?
2. How often does your congregation's board take time to reflect quietly before making decisions? Does someone intervene when people are talking past one another and invite a deeper kind of listening?
3. How could you initiate a conversation about how your faith community could be a refuge or sanctuary of peacefulness for those needing more calm in their lives?
4. Do the lay and clergy leaders in your congregation avail themselves of sabbath time on a weekly and annual basis? Does your congregational budget reflect giving a sabbatical to clergy and program staff?
5. Often religious education for children and youth are designed to keep participants busy. What steps would need to be taken to build in time for developing meditation or for nurturing silence or greater reflection?

Chapter 6

Power (Agency)

Don't ask yourself what the world needs, ask yourself what makes you come alive. And then go and do that. Because what the world needs is people who have come alive.
—*Howard Washington Thurman, 1899–1981*[1]

As you read the poetry and scripture in this chapter, I invite you to be aware of your own power or agency—your ability to be who God created you to be in all your glory, and your ability to do all that God created you to do. You may remember specific times when you acted with power and competence. You may also remember a sense of agency that did not seem to be anchored in any particular outcome.

Allow yourself to abide in your power. Befriend the feelings that arise.

Stop reading at any point to write in a journal or to call a companion to read a passage aloud. Recall your own favorite poems, stories, and Scripture passages that relate to sadness.

As a free writing exercise, write for five minutes beginning with one of these prompts:

I am powerful when . . .
or
Power is . . .

Well, children, where there is so much racket there must be something out of kilter. I think that 'twixt the negroes of the South and the women at the North, all talking about rights, the white men will be in a fix pretty soon. But what's all this here talking about?

That man over there says that women need to be helped into carriages, and lifted over ditches, and to have the best place everywhere. Nobody ever helps me into carriages, or over mud-puddles, or gives me any best place! And ain't I a woman? Look at me! Look at my arm! I have ploughed and planted, and gathered into barns, and no man could head me! And ain't I a woman? I could work as much and eat as much as a man—when I could get it—and bear the lash as well! And ain't I a woman? I have borne thirteen children, and seen most all sold off to slavery, and when I cried out with my mother's grief, none but Jesus heard me! And ain't I a woman?

Then they talk about this thing in the head; what's this they call it? [member of audience whispers, "intellect"] That's it, honey. What's that got to do with women's rights or negroes' rights? If my cup won't hold but a pint, and yours holds a quart, wouldn't you be mean not to let me have my little half measure full?

Then that little man in black there, he says women can't have as much rights as men, 'cause Christ wasn't a woman! Where did your Christ come from? Where did your Christ come from? From God and a woman! Man had nothing to do with Him.

If the first woman God ever made was strong enough to turn the world upside down all alone, these women together ought to be able to turn it back, and get it right side up again! And now they is asking to do it, the men better let them.

Obliged to you for hearing me, and now old Sojourner ain't got nothing more to say.
—*Sojourner Truth, 1797–1883,*
Ain't I a Woman? A Play Adaptation by Kirsten Childs[2]

⁓

The Growing Edge
All around worlds are dying out, new worlds are being born.
All around us life is dying and life is being born:
The fruit ripens on the tree;
The roots are silently at work in the darkness of the earth
Against the time when there shall be new leaves, fresh blossoms,
    green fruit.
Such is the growing edge!
It is the extra breath from the exhausted lung,
The one more thing to try when all else has failed,
The upward reach of life when weariness closes in upon all endeavor.
This basis of hope in moments of despair,
The incentive to carry on when times are out of joint
And men have lost their reason; the source of confidence
When worlds crash and dreams whiten into ash.
The birth of a child—life's most dramatic answer to death—
This the Growing Edge incarnate,
Look well to the growing edge!
—*Howard Thurman*[3]

⁓

You see things; and you say "Why?" But I dream of things that never were; and say "Why not?"
—*George Bernard Shaw, 1856–1950, Back to Methuselah*[4]

⁓

We who lived in concentration camps can remember the men who walked through the huts comforting others, giving away their last piece of bread. They may have been few in number, but they offer sufficient proof that everything can be taken from a man but one thing: the last of the human freedoms—to choose one's attitude in any given set of circumstances, to choose one's own way.
—*Viktor Frankl, 1905–97, Man's Search for Meaning*[5]

From there he set out and went away to the region of Tyre. He entered a house and did not want anyone to know he was there. Yet he could not escape notice, but a woman whose little daughter had an unclean spirit immediately heard about him, and she came and bowed down at his feet. Now the woman was a Gentile, of Syrophoenician origin. She begged him to cast the demon out of her daughter. He said to her, "Let the children be fed first, for it is not fair to take the children's food and throw it to the dogs." But she answered him, "Sir, even the dogs under the table eat the children's crumbs." Then he said to her, "For saying that, you may go—the demon has left your daughter." So she went home, found the child lying on the bed, and the demon gone.

—*Mark 7:24–30*

And Mary said,
"My soul magnifies the Lord,
and my spirit rejoices in God my Savior,
for he has looked with favor on the lowliness of his servant.
Surely, from now on all generations will call me blessed;
for the Mighty One has done great things for me,
and holy is his name.
His mercy is for those who fear him
from generation to generation.
He has shown strength with his arm;
he has scattered the proud in the thoughts of their hearts.
He has brought down the powerful from their thrones,
and lifted up the lowly;
he has filled the hungry with good things,
and sent the rich away empty.
He has helped his servant Israel,
in remembrance of his mercy,
according to the promise he made to our ancestors,
to Abraham and to his descendants for ever."

—*Luke 1:46–55*

When he came to Nazareth, where he had been brought up, he went to the synagogue on the sabbath day, as was his custom. He stood up to read, and the scroll of the prophet Isaiah was given to him. He unrolled the scroll and found the place where it was written:

The Spirit of the Lord is upon me,
because he has anointed me
to bring good news to the poor.
He has sent me to proclaim release to the captives
and recovery of sight to the blind,
to let the oppressed go free,
to proclaim the year of the Lord's favor.
And he rolled up the scroll, gave it back to the attendant, and sat
down. The eyes of all in the synagogue were fixed on him. Then
he began to say to them, "Today this scripture has been fulfilled
in your hearing." All spoke well of him and were amazed at the
gracious words that came from his mouth. They said, "Is not this
Joseph's son?"

                                        —*Luke 4:16–22*

Very truly, I tell you, the one who believes in me will also do the
works that I do and, in fact, will do greater works than these,
because I am going to the Father. I will do whatever you ask in
my name, so that the Father may be glorified in the Son. If in my
name you ask me for anything, I will do it.

                                        —*John 14:12–14*

Finally, beloved, whatever is true, whatever is honorable, whatever
is just, whatever is pure, whatever is pleasing, whatever is com-
mendable, if there is any excellence and if there is anything worthy
of praise, think about these things. Keep on doing the things that
you have learned and received and heard and seen in me, and the
God of peace will be with you. I can do all things through him
who strengthens me.

                                        —*Philippians 4:8–9, 13*

Claiming Power

When I was a very small child, one of my favorite stories was *The
Little Engine That Could.* An early published version of the story
appeared in the *New York Tribune* on April 8, 1906, as part of
a sermon by Rev. Charles S. Wing. The version I read was writ-

ten by Watty Piper, a pen name for Arnold Munk, who was the owner of the publishing firm Platt and Munk.[6] The story is about a little, blue railroad switch engine whose job is to move a few cars on and off the switches. One morning a long train of freight cars asks a large engine to take it over a high hill. The big engine refuses, saying it is too difficult. After several other large engines also refuse, the train asks the little switch engine to pull it up the grade and over to the other side. "I think I can" is the response of the tiny locomotive as it couples onto the train. Along the way, the little blue engine stops to help stranded dolls and other toys make their way onto to the train, over the mountain, and into the city to awaiting children. All the way up the steep grade the little engine puffs, "I—think—I—can, I—think—I—can." And on its way down, it celebrates its ability by saying, "I thought I could, I thought I could."

This is a *powerful* story. It is a story of confidence, albeit, a bit tentative at first. It is a story that does not shame or blame others. It is a story about anticipated success and accomplishment. Over the years, I have loved reading the story to my own children and others who visited our home. For me, it exemplifies what it means to be or feel powerful. This is not about coercive power over another being. It does not rely on the dynamic of *better than* versus *less than*. The story is about one's own confidence and ability.

When I visit congregations that are struggling with finances and membership, and thus often struggling with their own self-image, I often wonder how their circumstances might change, if after taking a somber look at themselves, they were to read *The Little Engine That Could* and take on its attitude of confident, steady struggle. Over the past thirty-plus years of consulting, I have witnessed struggling congregations of all sizes and with all variety of problems. The difference between those that succeed, both on their terms and by many external measurements, and those that do not succeed correlates, in my experience, not so much with the quality of their resources or the wisdom of their strategic plans but rather with their sense of power.[7] Granted, the greater the resources and the better the planning, the more likely feeling powerful will gain some traction. And still, I'd bet on the little engine, which genuinely thinks it can pull the load, over the big locomotive with all the resources, the one that can't be bothered or deems the work too hard.

Over the past few years, I have grown to be quite a good cook. At times, I have even been tempted to paraphrase the famous French philosopher René Descartes (1596–1650): "I cook, therefore I am." When my children were small and I was getting bored with "white meals" (pasta, potatoes, bread, pasta, milk, did I mention pasta?) we were eating all too often, I challenged myself to come up with a new meal every week. Sometimes I cooked from a recipe I found in a cookbook or the Wednesday newspaper. Other times I tried to imitate a meal I had enjoyed at a restaurant. Sometimes I just made it up. As I increased my repertoire, my spouse started giving me cookbooks, thinking that I might enjoy them and hoping to encourage what was becoming a gastronomical benefit to both of us as well as our daughters. I can honestly say now that most people who have dinner at our home are quite pleased with their meal, if somewhat surprised by my growing expertise. For me this is a personal example of feeling powerful in an area that I grew into. I wasn't born a chef, and though our family ate fairly healthy meals, my parents weren't great cooks. You might say my inheritance was meager when it came to preparing fine meals. But one day "I thought I could." I had a sense of agency, born of only a little desperation! This agency, this sense of feeling or being powerful, started small. And it does not require being competitive (unless I decide to audition for *Iron Chef*). It does not necessitate having power *over* another person. It is not part of the better-than, less-than dynamic.

If we turn to the Scriptures, we can see contrasting stories of power. In some stories, power is *power over* others. It is oppressive, competitive, zero-sum-game power. We read, for instance, about the disciples fighting over who is the greatest (Mark 9:33–41) or the sibling struggles of Cain and Abel (Gen. 4:1–16), Jacob and Esau (Gen. 27:1–45), or the prodigal son and his brother (Luke 15:11–32).

By contrast, the Scriptures also include stories of being or feeling powerful in one's own right, not at the expense of another. The story of the Syrophoenician woman (Mark 7:24–30) and the Samaritan woman at the well (John 4:1–42) are examples of powerful women, women who sense the ability and competence given them by God, even in a male-dominated culture. These women engage Jesus from a place of integrity and confidence. They are not interested in dominance or competition. They want to foster their own competence and share power or knowledge with others—the first woman with her child and the Samaritan woman with the village. This form of power sharing is often referred to as *power with*.

Stimulus →	Feeling →	Message →	Need or Response
Sense of worth or determination; anticipated success	**POWERFUL**	I am competent. I am able.	Continue to foster my own competence and to empower others.

The *powerful* family of feelings includes confident, worthwhile, successful, respected, and faithful. These feelings are stimulated by a sense of one's worth or capability. When I am deeply aware that I am a child of God, a being made in God's own image, I feel powerful, confident in who I am. I sense my agency, or some might say, God's agency in and through me. Sometimes this feeling of power is accompanied by a sense of anticipated accomplishment, such as finishing a major project at work or cooking a wonderful meal for guests. I feel powerful when I have done everything to prepare for a meeting and anticipate that it will go well for everyone. Power is about the ability to be what I want to be or to do want I want to do. It is important to notice that feeling powerful here does not mean I exercise power over or dominate others. When I feel powerful, the message is "I am competent," and the need is to "Keep on keeping on!" That is, the feeling is telling me to continue being who I am at this moment or doing what I am doing.

How Power Shows Up in the Body

Power may be the most difficult feeling to describe physically. Often people think of power, competence, or confidence as more mental than emotional. Even the mantra of *The Little Engine That Could* is "I *think* I can." Yet if we pay close attention, we can become aware that the feeling of power resonates in our bodies. For me, I have a sense of standing taller, of my feet being more grounded, my body more balanced, literally. I sense a clarity of thought. This is not about the content of what I am thinking, but rather I sense that there aren't any cobwebs interfering with the *process* of my decision making. I also feel adaptable, flexible. I have a sense that my various body parts can move as they need to. I feel fluid.

I want to contrast this sense of ability to be or to do, this sense of *power with*, to the feeling of *power over*, which has bodily connections as well. When I am feeling power over or dominance, my body is more tense, less flexible. I am more likely to be rigid than limber. I have a sense of my mental apparatus being more closed down, more tightly focused, less adaptable. I am more positioned to say no than to say yes or "We'll see."

Power and Connection

In discussing some of the Scripture passages above, I distinguished between dominant, oppressive *power over* and more collaborative, expansive *power with*. Jean Baker Miller and Joyce F. Fletcher offer great examples of how feeling and being powerful can deepen relationships.[8] Both women are pioneers in the field of relational-cultural theory. Miller has identified five "good things" or characteristics about relationships: zest, power and effectiveness, knowledge, a sense of worth, and a desire for more connection. By power and effectiveness, she means that in a good relationship, you feel "empowered to act *right in the immediate relationship—in this interplay, itself.*"[9] This power is not power over another person. It is relational—the power you share with another person. *Power with* enables a person who is in need (for example, someone who is about to lose a loved one or someone who is struggling with cancer) to feel heard and to be even more able to respond. In the mutuality of the relationship, both parties allow themselves to be changed. Neither person is in control. Each person feels enlarged, empowered, and more real. Each has a deeper knowledge of herself and of the other. Each desires more connection. This is how the Syrophoenician woman and the woman at the well responded in relationship to Jesus and he to them.

Power and Gender

While congregations frequently profess to uphold the dignity of every human being or to exercise a preferential option for the poor and marginalized, power is generally concentrated in a few leaders, frequently men, especially at the highest institutional levels, and usually in those who are theologically educated at a graduate level and ordained or in people who are materially wealthy. This discrepancy between the espoused mutuality theory and the hierarchical practice is often attributed to denominational polity or scriptural precedent. While it is true that women have become denominational leaders as well as pastors of very large congregations, the statistical odds are still in favor of men being in positions of leadership. Until the numbers are more balanced, speaking about the different ways women and men exercise power will be difficult, partly because the standard of measurement will remain how men perform. Women's behavior will be seen as exceptional or deviant.

I was recently consulting in a congregation where a female pastor's ministry of fourteen years was coming to an end. She was the first woman to be pastor of that church. In the hallway outside the sanctuary were more than twenty-five pictures of white male pastors. Her picture wasn't on the wall, presumably because she had to be dead or gone to be seen there. I had been hired to assist the church board and the congregation with a process of transition. The previous pastor's departure had been extremely problematic, and the current one was shaping up in some similar ways. In meeting with the board, I suggested that the pastor and board go through a process of naming affirmations, regrets or missed opportunities, learnings, and blessings. I suggested that a tenure of fourteen years must surely include many things for which the pastor could affirm the board and vice versa. And indeed that happened.

After several minutes, as the comments slowed, I intervened. I expressed my curiosity that no one spoke about gender. I mentioned the "rogues gallery," and several people laughed, mostly women. They knew immediately what I meant. I said that they might offer affirmations for the pastor that related to her gender, and for the board and congregation for facing into the newness and risks involved in changing literally hundreds of years of history. An older man beside me said, "What's gender got to do with it? It shouldn't make any difference whether our pastor is a man or a woman." A few people gasped, and one woman said, "It matters to me!"

Congregations have differing abilities and skills in discussing issues of power and gender. What was shocking in this situation was that no one felt comfortable broaching the subject at a time when I was being told by some members of the congregation (mostly men) that this pastor's style of leadership was no longer what was needed. I intuitively suspected they meant that it was time to hire another man as rector.

Having been in college and graduate school in the 1960s and '70s when it seemed as though everyone was talking about gender, I have a sense that faith communities, as well as North American culture in general, have regressed in our ability to speak meaningfully about leadership, power, and gender. Some of the reflection questions at the end of this section will invite you to reflect on your experience about how feeling powerful might be experienced differently by women and by men. To facilitate that discussion, I turn now to the distinction between power over and power with.

Powerful Communities

Joyce Fletcher, professor of management at the Center for Gender in Organizations at Simons Graduate School of Management and a Senior Research Scholar of the Jean Baker Miller Training Institute at Wellesley College, applies the insights of relational-cultural theory in corporate settings. Her work can provide insights into how *power with* can operate in congregations. Fletcher believes that the work of valuing, supporting, and deepening relationships has historically fallen to women, whose strategic and effective contributions to the system are then "disappeared" or belittled as being merely "nice" instead of effective or powerful. To give proper value to their contributions, she suggests strategies built upon the significance of the relational work. According to Fletcher, leadership, decision making, and organizational learning have historically been defined by those with the most power in the system and have been put into practice in a way that generally favors those who hold power. In contrast, she suggests team building, mutual empowerment, and fluid expertise (in which "power and expertise shift from one party to the other, not only over time but in the course of one interaction") as alternative strategies for leading and learning, where power is more widely distributed and mutually shared.[10]

Many organizations assume that knowledge and expertise are concentrated in a few people in positions of power at the top of the organization chart. When the culture of an organization allows people to admit their lack of knowledge and their need for help, it creates a greater opportunity for technology transfer, mutual empowerment, and organizational change. Congregations with robust lay leadership in decision making and ministry will more likely mentor people into roles of leadership, thus diminishing burnout and stagnation. No one, clergy or layperson, is assumed to be irreplaceable. The contributions of all, small and great, are valued. This is what the apostle Paul has in mind when he writes to the Corinthian community about all being valued parts of the one body (1 Cor. 12:12–31).

Finally, many organizations also show a strong bias toward "rational" thinking, excluding feelings as an empirical source of data about what is happening and needs to happen in an organization. Calling attention to this bias can be a way of integrating emotional literacy and affective competence into the organization's way of operating. This means giving *power* or *agency* full weight as an emotional leadership quality.

Resources

Fletcher, Joyce. *Disappearing Acts: Gender, Power, and Relational Practice at Work.* Cambridge, MA: MIT Press, 1999. Fletcher describes how emotional competence and relational behaviors get "disappeared" in the workplace. She identifies strategies for effectively implementing more collaborative leadership and for valuing emotional competence within organizations.

Gilligan, Carol, and David A. J. Richards. *The Deepening Darkness: Patriarchy, Resistance, and Democracy's Future.* Cambridge, MA: Harvard University Press, 2009. Psychologist Gilligan and lawyer Richards talk about how art, religion, psychology, and literature can be sources of resistance to patriarchy.

Miller, Jean Baker. *Toward a New Psychology of Women.* Boston: Beacon Press, 1976. Psychiatrist Miller, considered the founder of relational-cultural theory, describes a way of practicing psychology that takes seriously the experience of women (therapists and clients).

Packer, Tina, and John O. Whitney. *Power Plays: Shakespeare's Lessons in Leadership and Management.* New York: Simon & Schuster, 2000. Shakespearean actor and director Packer and business executive Whitney explores the bard's plays for examples that challenge and inspire corporate leadership.

Robb, Christina E. *This Changes Everything: The Relational Revolution in Psychology.* New York: Farrar, Straus, & Giroux, 2006. The Pulitzer Prize-winning journalist describes the birth and history of relational-cultural psychology, as well as its theory, against the backdrop of the civil rights movement, the women's movement, and the protest against the Vietnam War.

Sprinkle, Stephen V. "In the Market of the Cupid Vendors: Fou-
cauldian and Post-Foucauldian Critiques of Ecclesial Power and
Leadership." *Journal of Religious Leadership* 6, no. 2 (Fall 2007).
Disciple of Christ minister and seminary professor Sprinkle offers
provocative critiques of church leadership based too heavily on a
power-over model.

Reflection Questions

Personal Level

1. When did you feel powerful as a child? Who supported
   your sense of competence and in what areas?
2. Whom did you perceive as having the most power in
   your family of origin? How would you describe that
   power? Power over? Power with? Enabling power?
3. Describe a time when you felt you were becoming powerless, when you felt you were losing your agency.
4. Where do you feel power or agency in your current community of faith?
5. Where would you like to have more power, influence,
   agency in your current community of faith?

Congregational Level

1. Who gets to make decisions in your congregation? Who
   has authority to preach and to lead the community in
   prayer?
2. Which texts and hymns are held sacred? What language is
   used to conduct worship? What styles of music reflect the
   cultures of the people?
3. How would decisions be different if ensuring and deepening connections among members, even among those

who most disagree, were the primary value in your congregation?

4. How transparent are the power relationships in your congregation?

5. To what extent are people in your faith community able to express being powerful and to encourage others to feel powerful?

Chapter 7

Joy

All who joy would win must share it. Happiness was born a Twin.
—*Lord Byron, 1788–1824, Don Juan*[1]

As you read the poetry and scripture in this chapter, I invite you to be aware of your own joy—at seeing a newborn babe, hearing your name called by a loved one, baking a wonderful loaf of bread, sinking a long put, experiencing God's nearness.

Allow yourself to abide in your joy. Befriend the warmth and pleasure that arise.

Stop reading at any point to write in a journal or to call a companion to read a passage aloud. Recall your own favorite poems, stories, works of art, and Scripture passages that relate to joy.

As a free writing exercise, write for five minutes beginning with one of the following prompts:

I am joyful when . . .
or
Joy is . . .

Sonnet 8
Music to hear, why hear'st thou music sadly?
Sweets with sweets war not, joy delights in joy:
Why lov'st thou that which thou receiv'st not gladly,
Or else receiv'st with pleasure thine annoy?
If the true concord of well-tuned sounds,
By unions married, do offend thine ear,
They do but sweetly chide thee, who confounds
In singleness the parts that thou shouldst bear.
Mark how one string, sweet husband to another,
Strikes each in each by mutual ordering;
Resembling sire and child and happy mother,
Who, all in one, one pleasing note do sing:
Whose speechless song being many, seeming one,
Sings this to thee: "Thou single wilt prove none."
—*William Shakespeare*[2]

God's Grandeur
The world is charged with the grandeur of God.
It will flame out, like shining from shook foil;
It gathers to a greatness, like the ooze of oil
Crushed. Why do men then now not reck his rod?
Generations have trod, have trod, have trod;
And all is seared with trade; bleared, smeared with toil;

And wears man's smudge and shares man's smell: the soil
Is bare now, nor can foot feel, being shod.
And for all this, nature is never spent;
There lives the dearest freshness deep down things;
And though the last lights off the black West went
Oh, morning, at the brown brink eastward, springs—
Because the Holy Ghost over the bent
World broods with warm breast and with ah! bright wings.
            —*Gerard Manley Hopkins*[3]

Exultation is the going
Of an inland soul to sea—
Past the Houses—
Past the Headlands—
Into deep Eternity—
Bred as we, among the mountains,
Can the sailor understand
The divine intoxication
Of the first league out from Land?
                —*Emily Dickinson*[4]

You stand at the seashore perhaps knee-deep in water observing
    the skies, the wide horizons, the openness.
You listen to the birds; they are singing for their own joy.
You listen and the sounds do something to you.
It is happening.
The only requirement is to be there.
In the simplicity of your being, communion takes place.
You are not seeking, but something is bestowed on you, something
touches you at all levels.
        —*Vimala Thakar, The Eloquence of Living*[5]

There is no true joy in a life lived closed up in the little shell of the
self. When you take one step to reach out to people, when you
meet with others and share their thoughts and sufferings, infinite
compassion and wisdom well up within your heart. Your life is
transformed.
            —*Daisaku Ikeda*[6]

"For as soon as I heard the sound of your greeting, the child in my
    womb leaped for joy. And blessed is she who believed that there
    would be a fulfillment of what was spoken to her by the Lord."
And Mary said,
"My soul magnifies the Lord,
and my spirit rejoices in God my Savior,
for he has looked with favor on the lowliness of his servant.
Surely, from now on all generations will call me blessed;
for the Mighty One has done great things for me,
and holy is his name."
                    —*Luke 1:44–49*

As the Father has loved me, so I have loved you; abide in my love.
If you keep my commandments, you will abide in my love, just
as I have kept my Father's commandments and abide in his love.
I have said these things to you so that my joy may be in you, and
that your joy may be complete.
                    —*John 15:9–11*

Jesus knew that they wanted to ask him, so he said to them, "Are
you discussing among yourselves what I meant when I said, 'A little
while, and you will no longer see me, and again a little while, and
you will see me'? Very truly, I tell you, you will weep and mourn,
but the world will rejoice; you will have pain, but your pain will turn
into joy. When a woman is in labor, she has pain, because her hour
has come. But when her child is born, she no longer remembers
the anguish because of the joy of having brought a human being
into the world. So you have pain now; but I will see you again, and
your hearts will rejoice, and no one will take your joy from you.
On that day you will ask nothing of me. Very truly, I tell you, if
you ask anything of the Father in my name, he will give it to you.
Until now you have not asked for anything in my name. Ask and
you will receive, so that your joy may be complete."
                    —*John 16:19–24*

At that time the disciples came to Jesus and asked, "Who is the
greatest in the kingdom of heaven?" He called a child, whom he
put among them, and said, "Truly I tell you, unless you change
and become like children, you will never enter the kingdom of
heaven. Whoever becomes humble like this child is the greatest in

the kingdom of heaven. Whoever welcomes one such child in my name welcomes me."

—*Matthew 18:1–5*

Made for Joy

As infants we naturally express feelings that are congruent with events or situations that stimulate us. We are created that way. Under normal circumstances, before social conditioning enters the picture, our emotional software functions automatically, and the feeling that arises gives us a message about what we need. In Matthew's Gospel, Jesus's invitation to change and become like children is introduced with the question about who is the greatest, and the parallel passages in Mark and Luke start with the disciples fighting about who is the greatest. It may be that this passage is about humility, seeing or valuing ourselves as who we are (cognitive realm) and behaving in ways that are appropriate (behavioral realm). But what if we approached this passage from the affective realm? What if Jesus were urging us to be in touch with what our feelings are telling us about what we need?

While I believe that as adults we would all do well to "become like children" in regard to recognizing and attending to all our emotions, I want to focus on the feeling of joy, which for many people may seem most characteristic of children. I think joy comes from a sense of awe and wonder. It corresponds to an inner gratitude. When I am grateful and joyful, I am connected to myself and to the Divine—*even if* I am not consciously aware of that connection or attending to it at the time. When I am feeling joy, it is also easier to be connected to others and harder to be critical, argumentative, or nasty.

When our two daughters were in grade school, if their mother, Chris, and I got into an argument at the dinner table or starting bickering about something, Susannah would stand behind Chris and Rachel would stand behind me. Before Chris and I could notice them, one daughter would begin, "Oh sugarplum honeybunch, I love you so much." The other would respond with, "Sweetie-pie lovey-doll, you mean so much to me. I treasure everything you say." In no time, the four of us were laughing uncontrollably, even as the girls attempted to maintain the sweet chatter. I don't remember the content of any of the arguments that provoked my daughters to initiate their ad-libbed voice-overs, but I do remember the laughter and joy they generated. Their zany antics were the stimulus that brought joy and laughter out of a tense situation. I am sure they tried more rational approaches, such as asking us to stop fighting—probably even using the exact words we had employed to stop their bickering with one another. Maybe that didn't work because they were children, acting like adults, urging us to "grow up." Probably they were just being their own creative kid-selves. Whatever was behind their behavior, it worked very effectively.

When I think about the bickering of some congregational boards and committees, I am reminded of the way my wife and I were spatting. Generally, my solution to conflict in groups is to teach guidelines for talking and working across differences.[7] But as I recall what worked in my own family, I sometimes wonder if a quicker way to halt bickering, hurtful behavior would be to introduce unexpected humor—to foster a move to gratitude and joy.

My wife and I recently got a new puppy. It was my wife's idea. Our loving pound puppy of fourteen years had died eighteen months before, and I suspect I was still sad about losing her. "It's not a convenient time," I said. "I've got this book to write and way too much work to do at school. And what about the trips we plan to take?" But she'd not listen to my misgivings. In the end, it was easier for me to give in.

I had forgotten what joy a puppy can bring out in me. Others have probably written eloquently about the way four-legged creatures have the ability to bring joy to one's life. It's no wonder dogs are now being used as therapy animals in hospitals, nursing homes, and retirement communities. Perhaps they bring out the child in each of us, the joy of life lived in the moment.

Stimulus →	Feeling →	Message →	Need or Response
Inner gratitude; awe, wonder	**JOY**	I am excited, happy.	Continue to relish the joy and share it as appropriate.

The *joyful* family of feelings includes excited, energetic, playful, creative, sensuous, optimistic, and hopeful. Inner gratitude and a sense of wonder or awe can stimulate joy. When I feel joy, I simply want to relish it for a while. But most often, joy longs to be shared. Thus the response to joy is both to relish it and to find appropriate ways to share it, to find others who will enjoy being part of my delight. In situations where few people are expressing joy, one needs to exercise care in how much joy and with whom one shares it. If the culture of the family, group, or community is joy deprived and thus joy avoidant, the danger is that people will want to throw a wet blanket on the one expressing joy. The situation may be similar to a person who has been starving from hunger: it is necessary to begin nourishing the person with small amounts of nutritious food. It may be hard for joy-starved people to see that joy is not phony or a zero-sum game. This is especially true if they have had long draughts of sadness or depression or if the family or community has a history of serious domestic or substance abuse.

How Joy Shows Up in the Body

Joy is often accompanied by a smile; the cheeks and the corners of one's mouth rise up. Joy is associated with inner and outer warmth. We often take in a deep breath when we first experience joy. Joy can be the response to a pleasant thought or memory. It can also enter through any of the five senses: hearing beautiful music or a friend's voice, feeling a caring touch or sensual pleasure, smelling a rose, tasting fresh fruit, seeing a loved one, a beautiful landscape, or a smiling baby.

Joy and Connection

Connection seems to be built into joy. While I can feel peaceful all by myself and frequently prefer the peacefulness of solitude, joy is a feeling that I almost feel compelled to share. As Lord

Byron put, "All who joy would win must share it. Happiness was born a Twin."

Humor is frequently linked to joy, but humor at the expense of an individual or group does not bring true joy. Finding ways that we can laugh at ourselves and life's circumstances without shaming or belittling others offers opportunities for joy that can be shared.

About a year ago I gathered with four colleagues from across the country to write the final report on more than three years of research about cross-cultural learning for divinity students in international and domestic immersion experiences. We worked very hard for two full days, with appropriate breaks and intermittent humor. As we celebrated over dinner, an opening occurred and I told a fictitious story, a joke really, that depended upon someone asking just the right question at the end of the story. Someone bit. I delivered the punch line and as the others moaned, realizing they had fallen for my bogus story, I went into uncontrollable laughter. The joke wasn't really *that* funny. I managed to blurt out that it had been twenty-five years since I had told that joke. Before long, though, all of us were laughing irrepressibly. No sooner would we start to become quiet, then someone would begin to laugh again—each of us in our own unique and, I believe, primitive style.

The work we had produced together was significant and brought us quite close together. We enjoyed the ways in which we challenged each other intellectually, and at times each of us commented on the joy of how we worked in challenging and collaborative ways. But that night of laughing unleashed a new and deeper dimension of bonding.

Joy and Gender

I sometimes wonder if what brings joy to men and to women differs. Do men feel more joy in accomplishing tasks and women more joy in relationships? I want to say a resounding "No!" And yet, there does seem to be some truth in the fact that men and women are conditioned differently about what they should strive for, and men and women are rewarded unequally for pursuing careers and relationships. My suspicion is not that we are created to respond differently to the same stimuli but that over time we receive messages about what will make us happy, and for one reason or another we begin to internalize those messages and construct our lives and our notions of happiness around the messages we have internalized. For me, the significance of possible gender differences regarding joy is not about how we are hardwired or even how we have been shaped. Rather, the invitation to consider gender and joy is to discuss (as in the reflection questions) what it is that brings us joy or pleasure and further to support and reward one another when we are acting against the stereotype. For example, we might praise boys who seek to value maintaining a relationship more than insisting on the "rules of the game." Or we could praise girls who strive for excellence in math or a sport, even if it begins to challenge a friendship or inclusion in a certain circle of peers. The point is not to set up either-or dichotomies but to notice if there are differences along gender lines and to create space for those differences.

This invitation to notice the differences in what brings us joy applies to all the emotions, as does the encouragement to appreciate and reward people who are expressing emotions congruent for them, even if their expression does not fit a gender, racial, ethnic, or cultural stereotype. The more room we make for people to express individual feelings, the more each of us will feel free to express what is true for us in any given situation.

Joyful Communities

What characterizes a joyous congregation? I once asked a group of pastors that question, and one responded, "I really don't know, but I'd be suspicious of being in one." When I think of congregations or organizations I know that have been genuinely joyous, I do not have in mind a group of people blithely singing tunes from *The Sound of Music* or *Mary Poppins*. Deep congregational joy may be more like the *zest* that psychologist Jean Baker Miller speaks about as one of the five good things that characterize healthy relationships. Zest, according to Miller, has to do with being fully engaged in the relationship.[8] It means being alive to what is happening in oneself and in the other, and thus in the relationship between people. One can have a sense of zest even when comforting a friend who has just been widowed. While we might be reluctant to describe such a time as joyous, the quality of connection is such that the tragedy is held in a supportive relationship.

Joyous congregations are able to not take themselves too seriously. They are not focused only on the bottom line. All decisions are not about what is productive and effective. They are communities of people who like to waste time together. In a joyous congregation, both Mary and Martha are present, and Martha also sometimes doffs her apron and sits down with Jesus (Luke 10:38–42).

Another word for joy in this corporate sense is *vitality*. I have noticed a growing trend to speak about the viability and vitality of congregations. If viability answers the question "*Can* this faith community survive?" vitality is much more about "*Should* it survive?" or "What difference would it make if it did survive?" Of course, vitality is about much more than survival, just as joy is about more than breathing. Vitality is about exuberant physical, mental, and spiritual vigor; it is about a *meaningful* or *purposeful* existence.

While any congregation or community can be joyous or vital, many white people think of a visit to an African American or black church when asked if they have ever visited a joyous congregation. What comes to mind is the robust singing, the spontaneous amens and halleluiahs, the clapping and swaying. No doubt every racial, ethnic, and cultural variety of church has its deadly services. What leads some white people to associate black churches with joy, however, may be the deep engagement of nearly everyone in the congregation. The feeling of joy or vitality is infectious. As

Mark Twain wrote, "To get the full value of a joy, you must have someone to divide it with." Engaging in cross-cultural exchanges can open white Christians to experience exhilaration that they might not associate with church. In such cross-cultural situations, visitors should exercise caution in their interpretation of what is taking place if they do not know the history or the emotional nuances of the congregation.

As we contemplate joy, especially corporate joy, it is crucial to see the flip side of the coin. The deep joy of a black church is often a later chapter in the narrative of shared struggle and oppression. Gospel music and black spirituals come out of the faith experience of a people for whom viability or survival was the central issue. Real joy is an expression of a belief that God has led and will again lead God's people from slavery to freedom, from bondage to the promised land. For faith communities, joy comes from the lived experience of divine accompaniment.

The Jewish celebration of Simchat Torah, in the fall after Sukkot, is an example of community joy. The name of the festival literally means "rejoicing in the Torah." It celebrates the completion of the reading of the Torah cycle (the first five books of the Bible). But it means much more than that. The Jewish people are commanded to study the Torah every day and to read it publically on Shabbat. And for more than a thousand years it has been the custom on Simchat Torah to *dance* with the Torah—physically and emotionally tying the people to God's word and to one another. Furthermore, this celebration has a profoundly democratic character to it. Men, women, and children dance and process with the Torah, symbolizing that the Torah belongs to the entire people, scholars and laypeople, children, women, and men. Again, the joy is not an accidental, fleeting whim; rather, it is grounded in a communal identity of being led and accompanied by the Divine.

Most of the time we think of feelings as responses to discrete, in-the-moment stimuli. And so it is with the experience of joy. At the same time, there is a dimension of joy, peace, and power that has deep roots, especially when we consider the spiritual significance of these feelings or how they are connected not simply to our bodily sensations but also to our faith. Said another way, for those who believe in a Creator and One to whom we will return or be reunited, the very way we are constructed as feeling-responsive beings means that our connection to the Source of Life is not only through our minds but also in the very ways that our bodies and emotions function. This does not mean that we are always aware of this connection. The stimulus → feeling → message → need or response dynamic operates even when we are not consciously aware of it, however. And as people of faith, it is possible to reflect theologically on how this mechanism works and how we are connected through our feelings to the source of joy, peace, and power.

The ground and arc of joy to which I am referring here—the sense that I have been created in joy and will ultimately return to a state of joy—is a basic tenet of Buddhism. It is summed up rather simply in the teaching of Daisaku Ikeda: "The joy of life is to be found not by evading life's sufferings but by grappling with them to the finish. True happiness is not born of escape; ecstasy based on delusion does not continue. Enlightenment comes from seeing the truth, no matter how unpleasant it may be."[9] For Christians, deep joy is not circumstantial. It is based on one's relationship with the Divine, who wishes for us better things than we can ask for or imagine. Joy that is a response to specific stimuli is connected to and a reminder of that deeper joy.

Resources

Buxbaum, Yitzhak. *Jewish Tales of Mystic Joy.* San Francisco: Jossey-Bass, 2002. A collection of tales of Jewish mysticism that inspires an appreciation of all that is good in one's life.

Tutu, Desmond M., and Mpho A. Tutu. *Made for Goodness: And Why This Makes All the Difference.* New York: HarperCollins Publishers, 2010. This book is about living with compassion, hope, and joy in the most difficult circumstances, such as the period of apartheid in South Africa.

Reflection Questions

Personal Level

1. What brought you joy as a child? Was your home one that nurtured joy and humor in you?
2. What did you do as a child that brought joy to significant elders in your life (parents, grandparents, teachers, pastors)?
3. When was the last time you had a really good belly laugh? What were the circumstances? Who were you with?
4. Do you have a habit or practice of seeking and nurturing joy in yourself? In others?

Congregational Level

1. Name a joyous community in which you have participated. Was the joy spontaneous or cultivated? What conditions allowed for the spontaneity? What was done to cultivate a sense of joy or vitality?
2. Where in your own faith community would a visitor be most likely to experience joy?
3. Are the children in your congregation encouraged and supported in their joy, vitality, and spontaneity? What opportunities are there for adults to learn from the children?
4. Are your congregation's board, finance committee, newcomers committee places where joy can be shared? Give examples.
5. How does your adult education program foster joy as well as stimulate people intellectually?
6. What liturgical celebrations (baptism, bris, bat or bar mitzvah, youth-led services, wedding, Welcome Home Sunday) and seasons of the church year open people to experience deep joy?

Chapter 8

Substitution and Projection

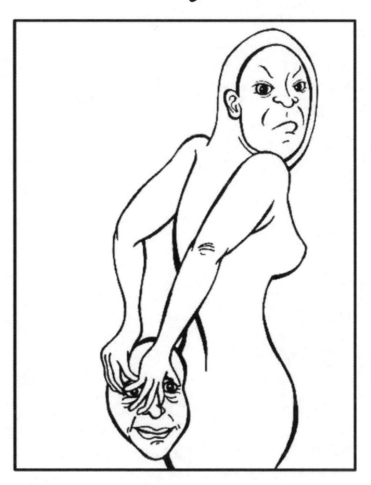

Be this the whetstone of your sword. Let grief
Convert to anger; blunt not the heart, enrage it.
—William Shakespeare, 1564–1616, Macbeth[1]

Now that you have an idea of the nuances of various key feelings and the messages they carry, let's look at the concepts of substitution and projection. In order to understand how we, as adults, substitute the expression of a feeling that was permitted in our family of origin for expression of a feeling that was prohibitted, we need to understand the idea of *congruence*. Congruence describes the chain of relationships from a stimulus (such as a loud, unexpected noise) to a bodily response (increased heart rate), to a feeling (fear), and to the message that feeling suggests (get safe or find support). This congruence is part of the programing with which we are born.

One difficulty many of us face as we try to become more in tune with our emotions is that we were raised to value only certain feelings. We were taught that only some feelings are legitimate to express. Often this message was "caught" rather than explicitly taught. It just wasn't okay to be sad as a child growing up. Sometimes we were told directly, "You have nothing to be sad about. Children all over the world are going hungry," or "Big boys don't cry!" In any case, we may have learned to substitute one feeling for another, usually without being aware that we are doing so. Such substitution is generally a habitual behavior that we learned for self-protection. When I first began to substitute a more acceptable feeling for the one congruent with the situation, it probably was not safe or sanctioned to express the natural feeling, that is, the feeling congruent with the stimulus. If I was a child and had no choice, the substitution may have been a matter of survival or a way to stay in the good graces of my parents or some other authority figure. The substitution becomes a problem if I unconsciously replace a congruent feeling with a substitute feeling when I am no longer in a context that requires me to substitute my feelings. For instance if a man realizes that adults cry when they are sad but he is still trying to act strong or powerful because he was socialized to do so, he will not likely receive comfort for a loss he is experiencing. When I substitute a feeling, perhaps out of habit, I get the response associated with the substituted feeling—instead of the response I really want or need, and associated with the feeling I have failed to recognize or express.

In my family of origin, feeling sad or scared was okay. Getting angry was not okay. My father was the only one who was allowed to get angry. When I experienced a boundary violation, I could be sad, even cry, and seek comfort, or I could be afraid and seek support and protection. I could not express anger that someone had come into my space or crossed an emotional boundary. This restriction meant that in my family, if I was angry, I had to substitute an acceptable feeling of sadness or fear. Thus, at the precise time I needed space or distance to reestablish boundaries, I had to give the message (through an expression of sadness or being scared) that I wanted someone to come closer to comfort or protect me.

This substitution pattern of sadness for anger is also common for many women. It becomes particularly problematic if a woman has experienced physical or emotional abuse. At precisely the time when she has a right to be angry and when anger would serve to create some distance from a controlling or abusive male colleague or superior, she may be acting, out of conditioning or habit, to express sadness, which may draw the offender closer in a kind of false comfort. The congruent emotion of anger carries the message, "Renegotiate boundaries and expectations" or perhaps more bluntly, "Back off and behave!" Recent research indicates a higher frequency of sexual abuse among men than has previously been reported.[2] For men, especially those who were not allowed to express anger in their families of origin and who were abused as children, this same substitution pattern is possible. They may be conditioned to express sadness or fear instead of anger.

In the case of the man who had been taught as a child to act powerful instead of being sad, the message he is accustomed to conveying is "I'm okay. I can handle it." People around him then are likely to come to the conclusion that he doesn't need anything, when what he may really need is to grieve and receive support for his grieving. His expression of control pushes others away precisely when he may want them to draw nearer. Substituting a more acceptable or more familiar feeling (powerful, competent) for the natural one here (sadness, grief) deprives him of what he needs and gives off a signal to others that is confusing or misleading, because it is not congruent with what is taking place.

In North America, anger deserves special attention regarding patterns of social conditioning and substitution. In general, only *white men* in North America are granted the right to legitimately express anger. First of all, this means that everyone else has to find another noncongruent emotion to substitute socially when they are feeling anger. Second, this means that white men learn to substitute anger for many other emotions, most especially for fear, sadness, and feeling powerful or competent in ways that could empower others. As a corollary, our culture says that men of color and all women and children are not permitted to express anger, because they are not supposed to be able to renegotiate boundaries, power relationships, or expectations. The cultural norms of society about who gets to make decisions play a role in which feelings various groups of people are allowed to express.

Projection

As we work to become more emotionally literate and affectively competent,[3] it is also important to notice how easily we tend to project our own feelings onto other people. The Bartimaeus passage in Mark's Gospel is one of my favorites, and it illustrates the projection of feelings. I also find it quite humorous.

> They came to Jericho. As he and his disciples and a large crowd were leaving Jericho, Bartimaeus son of Timaeus, a blind beggar, was sitting by the roadside. When he heard that it was Jesus of Nazareth, he began to shout out and say, "Jesus, Son of David, have mercy on me!" Many sternly ordered him to be quiet, but he cried out even more loudly, "Son of David, have mercy on me!" Jesus stood still and said, "Call him here." And they called the blind man, saying to him, "Take heart; get up, he is calling you." So throwing off his cloak, he sprang up and came to Jesus. Then Jesus said to him, "What do you want me to do for you?" The blind man said to him, "My teacher, let me see again." (Mark 10:46–51)

Bartimaeus is one of the least shy, least scared people in the Gospels. He is a blind beggar, a marginalized person on the edge of society, *sitting* by the side of the road. But don't be fooled. He is anything but passive. He is shouting, screaming, calling attention to himself, if not intentionally, then because he has no choice if he wants to get Jesus's attention. When ordered sternly to be quiet, he screams louder. I think of him as almost a poster boy for Dylan Thomas's poem "Do Not Go Gentle into That Good Night":

> Do not go gentle into that good night,
> Old age should burn and rave at close of day;
> Rage, rage against the dying of the light.[4]

But let's look at the crowd and the disciples. The crowd, and probably the disciples, want the beggar to be quiet. He is at best a distraction. My guess is that the disciples are tired and just want to get down the road to a spot where they can rest. But Jesus has other ideas. He tells the disciples to bring Bartimaeus to him. And here is where the humor—and the projection—come in. The disciples say to Bartimaeus: "Take heart; get up, he is calling you." The "Take heart" sounds a lot like "Have courage" or "Don't be afraid." Bartimaeus is not afraid; the disciples are. Bartimaeus doesn't need courage. After all, he's the one who has been shouting. It is the disciples who need the courage to make their way through the crowd to face this obstreperous, raging man. The disciples are clearly projecting their own fear. If only they could *see* their own emotion, their own fear. But an amazing miracle takes place. In spite of their fear and lack of awareness of their projection, Jesus turns to them and turns them into instruments of healing. They conduct Bartimaeus to Jesus, who gives him (and the disciples) sight!

Projection does not always have such a fortuitous outcome. Often when we, unawares, project our emotions onto someone else, we encounter outrage from them or at best denial. What we have projected, they assure us, does not belong to them. When we hear from another that the feeling we are attributing does not fit, it's best to back off and ask ourselves if we are the one with that feeling.

Because substitution is often deeply engrained and outside awareness, the process for all parties of discovering what emotions are present at a given time is delicate, especially when the situation is tense or the stakes are high. Curiosity about oneself and about the other trumps certainty and righteousness in these situations. Patience and willingness to enter into the practice of peeling back layers of meaning and engrained habits are called for.

Substitution Exercise

The following is an exercise to help you notice what patterns of substitution you may have learned as a child and then to examine whether you are living out the same pattern now as an adult. The exercise may also help you identify another substitution pattern— perhaps because something in your current community makes it unsafe or undesirable to express a certain emotion. Complete the exercise and share it with someone you trust to learn more about your tendencies to substitute. You might also compare your substitution pattern with the pattern of your siblings. They might fill out the chart differently from you.

Feelings as Messengers Exercise

1. Write one of the six feelings (peaceful, powerful, joyful, scared, mad, sad) in each the blanks on the next page. You may use a feeling more than once or not at all.

Family of Origin

A Feeling most allowed for you: _____

B Feeling least allowed for you: _____

S Substituted feeling: _____

Community I Am in Now

AN Feeling most allowed: _____

BN Feeling least allowed: _____

SN Substituted feeling: _____

2. When you look at your feeling patterns, what do you notice?

_____

_____

_____

_____

3. What similarities or differences do you notice in your early
   pattern and your pattern now?

_____

_____

_____

_____

4. Place the letters **A, B, S** and **AN, BN, SN** on the chart below, next to the feelings you have identified above. Draw an
   arrow from **B → S** and from **BN → SN.** These show your
   substitution patterns.

PEACEFUL   **SAD**

MAD   **POWERFUL**

JOYFUL   **SCARED**

You can find a completed sample exercise in appendix B. It shows
both an early substitution of expressing *sad* for feeling *mad* and a
current substitution of *sad* when not being able to express *powerful.* It's as though this person has an emotional default set to *sad.*

Chapter 9

Shame and Guilt

So what about *shame* and *guilt?* you may be asking. Where do they fit into this schema of emotions? Aren't they important?

I have no doubt that shame and guilt play significant roles in our individual and congregational lives. However, I have not included them as basic feelings, because I think they are more complicated, secondary emotions learned through socialization—as distinct from primary, universal responses to basic stimuli. Nevertheless, they are important because they interfere with deeper relationships and with accomplishing effective ministry. For those reasons and because they are not well understood, I want to discuss them briefly and point to a few resources for further study.

Clinical psychologist and United Methodist clergywoman Karen McClintock has written a profound and very readable book entitled *Shame-Less Lives, Grace-Full Congregations.* In it she makes an important distinction between guilt and shame. She says "guilt is the moral compass and corrective function in the psyche that leads us to notice when we have harmed others with our behavior. Shame, however, is the emotion of self-recrimination that is more likely to weigh us down than spur us to action."[1] According to McClintock, the purpose of guilt is to restore us to right relationship with another or others and with oneself.

Shame is a tricky word in English. It has an *intrapersonal* meaning: I have a sense of shame, disgust, or remorse when I feel I have *done* something wrong, when I have harmed another person or myself. Shame points to a word, thought, or action I regret. In this sense, *intra*personal shame is similar to guilt; it is about my own self-awareness and is usually used with the phrase "I have a sense of shame." Shame also has an *inter*personal meaning. When we shame others or are shamed by them, the injury moves beyond *behavior* toward one's very *being.* McClintock puts it this way: "While guilt says, 'I *made* a mistake,' shame says, 'I *am* a mistake.' Shame takes a behavior and slaps it onto my core personhood. I become my mistakes."[2] Here, and for the most part throughout her book, McClintock is speaking about interpersonal shame, which isolates and stigmatizes. Shame in this sense has no redeeming qualities.

McClintock's book is a treasury of personal stories from her experience as a pastor and a psychologist specializing in shame recovery. She devotes chapters to the dynamics of the shame-blame game, the debilitating effects of comparison shame and perfection shame, mitigating chronic illness shame, and reducing individual sexual shame. She describes how shame operates in congregations and how they can move toward becoming "grace-full" communities. On the individual level, she offers new scripts for those who live with shame and alternatives for using shaming language with others. On the corporate level, she talks about how secrets lead to shame and how congregations can offer "do overs" as a way of healing shame.[3] Individuals who struggle with guilt or shame will find McClintock's work clarifying and an aid for making personal changes. Congregations that are hoping to become more affectively competent, and especially those that have struggled with sexual or financial abuse, can use McClintock's book for discussion groups and to help leaders understand the implications of shame on their corporate life.

Corporate shame is not restricted to sexual or financial abuse or the secrets that congregations may have about clergy or lay leaders who are addicted to alcohol, drugs, or gambling. Shame also plays a large role in the struggle of faith communities as they try to become more multicultural. As a consultant and trainer working to promote a multicultural approach to reducing oppressive individual behaviors and practices and policies within communities, I have used this guideline for recognizing and valuing differences: "It's okay to disagree; it's not okay to shame, blame, or attack self or others."[4] Speaking of shame when setting guidelines for interaction draws attention to the fact that shame is related to the way we think about differences. Whether the differences have to do with race, class, age, gender, sexual identity or orientation, or any other variable, shame is about believing that what makes *another person* different makes that person *less than* me or my group. This shaming of another person is oppression.[5] In the case of internalized oppression, shame is my belief, or the way I was socialized to believe about myself, that *I* am (or *my group* is) less than others because what makes us different makes us less than. In its extreme form, we speak or act as though the other person's very *being* (or my own being, in internalized oppression) is not okay.

Shame and Transactional Analysis

As individuals and communities struggle to move from shame to grace, they might benefit from exploring some insights from transactional analysis. Transactional analysis theory talks about the need for all human beings to receive strokes. A stroke is a unit of recognition. Strokes can be positive or negative, and conditional or unconditional. We all need positive unconditional strokes—strokes for our being, such as "I love you" or "I think you're great." Conditional strokes (about what we do or have) give us feedback or provide course corrections. A positive conditional stroke might be "I liked your sermon or presentation" or "That shirt you are wearing is a great color on you." A negative conditional stroke might be "You are behind schedule on the project you agreed to work on." Negative conditional strokes are about behaviors that we can change and imply the possibility of a remedy or alteration. Negative *un*conditional strokes are about one's being: "I hate you" or "You are a loathsome person." This is shaming and has no redeeming characteristics. Hence the guideline I use in my consulting work: no shaming!

Many of us work, and often live, in stroke-deprived environments. Usually this means that we do not get as many positive strokes as we need. Generally, people need ten to twenty positive strokes for every negative stroke they receive. With more people working from home via the Internet, opportunities for both positive strokes and negative conditional strokes are often reduced, and when they come electronically, we experience them differently. They feel less personal. If I have been shamed, if my being has been attacked (by a negative unconditional stroke), and I live and work in a stroke-deprived setting, it will be hard to get the positive reinforcement needed to heal and to feel good about myself.[6] Communities of faith can provide people with positive (conditional and unconditional) strokes as well as teach people appropriate ways to give conditional negative strokes that will give people information about how their behaviors are coming across to others. A skill that is helpful for staff, interns, committee chairs, and volunteers is *giving and receiving feedback*,[7] which is another way to talk about the appropriate use of positive and negative conditional strokes. Greeting people as they enter worship or arrive for a meeting or an educational session is a way to give a positive stroke. The greeting of peace in Christian worship can be seen as giving positive *un*conditional strokes. The purpose of the generous and appropriate use of strokes and feedback is that refraining from shame (seen here as *un*conditional negative strokes) is not enough. We also need to build up a healthy stroke economy by using *positive un*conditional strokes and appropriate positive and negative conditional strokes. Building a healthy stroke economy will move us toward what McClintock calls grace-full congregations.

Shame and Guilt in a Wider Context

Most often we think about shame and guilt on an individual level. This is understandable, because we experience shame and guilt most directly on a personal level. Cultural theorists and anthropologists can add to our understanding of shame and guilt, because they look at a larger picture. They notice differences between men and women and people of different cultural or ethnic backgrounds. It is beyond the scope of this book to discuss the many cultural or anthropological approaches to guilt and shame. But it is important to learn to notice how our culture and the culture of other people affect the experience and understanding of shame and guilt.

Anthropologist Edward T. Hall sheds some light on the discussion of shame and guilt by looking broadly at cultures, rather than focusing on individuals. Hall initiated a discussion of "high-context" and "low-context" cultures with his 1976 book *Beyond Culture*.[8] Hall noticed that people of different cultures varied significantly regarding the number of words they used in routine communication and the specificity of those words. He used the word *context* to explain this difference. Context includes the depth of bonds between people, the culture's sense of time and how structured or flexible it is, the strength of boundaries between in-groups and out-groups, as well as the locus (within individuals or external to them) of control and attribution of failure.

For Hall, high-context cultures (for example, Native American, Asian, Middle Eastern, and African cultures) rely heavily on non-verbal communication and place great emphasis on word choice, since few words communicate a great deal in a strongly shared cultural context. He finds that high-context cultures have a strong sense of family and make a strong distinction between in-groups and out-groups. They have a higher commitment to long-term relationship than to task accomplishment. High-context cultures tend to be more homogeneous than low-context cultures. Time is open and flexible; process is more important than product. The emphasis on community or *inter*dependence might be summed up by the African notion of *ubuntu*, "I am what I am because of who we all are." These are also cultures where shame and honor play a major role in establishing and controlling "right" behavior. For instance, many Native American groups use shame (as distinct from corporal punishment) almost exclusively to discipline children. Because shame is used as a method for disciplining or controlling children (clear subordinates), not shaming adults or people seen as equals and allowing them to save face are extremely important in these cultures. For these peoples, shame and honor are more operative cultural factors than external laws and determining guilt or innocence.

By contrast, low-context cultures (for example, European and North American cultures) place greater emphasis on verbal communication than nonverbal and rely on lengthy and detailed communication with less emphasis on specific words. They have a strong sense of the individual, flexible and porous groupings, and more commitment to task accomplishment than deep or long-term relationships. Low-context cultures tend to be more diverse. Time is highly structured and organized; product is more important than process. *In*dependence ("pulling oneself up by one's own bootstraps") is emphasized more than community. In these cultures, external laws and guilt or innocence are more operative cultural controls than shame.

With globalization, a blending of these cultures is underway, and at the same time, significant tensions arise as people from distinct worldviews encounter one another with little understanding of the depth of differences. Cultural awareness is critical for international exchange. And as local communities within the United States become increasingly diverse culturally, awareness of cultural differences regarding shame and guilt is necessary in all our congregations.

Within seven miles of the mostly Jewish New England suburban town where I live is a community with a high percentage of Nigerian (mostly Ibo speaking) and West Indian people. My own town of eighteen thousand people has two mosques and a Hindu shrine, with people from multiple ethnic backgrounds, in addition to eight synagogues and about the same number of Christian churches. My interactions with people from a wide variety of cultures has made it clear to me that my notions of shame and guilt are heavily influenced by my white European ancestors and by my being male. Though I am not as clear how all my neighbors think about shame and guilt, I am aware that we do not share the same assumptions. Let me give an example.

Fifteen years ago my wife and I bought a twenty-three-year-old house. Within a year of purchasing it, the new coat of paint began to chip off, mostly on the sunbathed south and west sides of the house. I suspect this was because the house had originally been stained and not properly sanded or primed before the paint was applied. Over the past few years, the house has looked pretty shabby, and we are about to have it reshingled. A few white neighbors who recently saw a new roof go on the house even asked if this is the year for the house to be painted or resided. We took their question to be information seeking, not in any way shame or guilt inducing. They knew that we had been putting our daughters through college, and they probably shared our white, New England values of frugality. Contrast this situation with that of my African American neighbor, who lives less than three hundred yards away. He also put two daughters through college. This past spring as he prepared his house and yard for the younger daughter's outdoor graduation party, he had all the trim on his house painted, even though his house was much newer than mine and showed little flaking. He also had some landscaping done. As I reflect on our differences, I suspect that our different cultural assumptions and conditioning regarding shame had an effect on our decisions about the appearance of our houses. Because of my black neighbor's cultural context, he felt a higher sense of honor, influencing him to make his house look good for his daughter, his relatives, and their friends. He had a greater possibility of being shamed by guests from his own black community and even by white neighbors than I might have experienced. His internal sense of honor and avoidance of shame around the house only became apparent to me as I realized my own privilege as a white person meant that I am mostly immune to shame in this regard. My mostly white neighbors, no matter how disgusted they are with the peeling paint on my house, are not going to say that I am bringing down the real estate values in the neighborhood. They might say that to my black neighbor. So both my neighbor's own sense of honor and shame and the way power and privilege exist in US society lead us to different assumptions and behaviors.[9]

The point of this cultural digression is that shame takes on different meanings depending on the cultural context and the influence of cultural heritage on an individual. In extreme cases, public shame in a high-context culture can place the shamed person completely outside the community, and community is the only way in which one can understand one's identity—"I am who I am because of who we all are." Here shame is practically a death sentence. If I am who I am because of my community, being outside that group is not simply disorienting. I may in a significant way cease to exist because I am no longer among my people. They are absent to me. In low-context cultures, shame rarely functions as a death sentence—though the suicides of LGBT people rejected by their families might be an example to the contrary.

The example of suicides by LGBT people, including teens, who have been victims of repeated pernicious bullying brings us back to McClintock's notion that shame is an attack on a person's core being. This makes sense even in the low-context culture of North America. While shame is experienced as a more intrapsychic phenomenon—"I am a mistake"—it can still have a devastating effect. Because relationships in low-context cultures have less significance than in high-context cultures, if I believe that I *am* a mistake, I will not be able to rely much on support relationships to mitigate my sense of isolation. In my isolation I might think, "I am alone. I am a mistake. There is no hope for me." Shame and isolation are reasons for churches, synagogues, and mosques to move from shame-full communities to grace-full gatherings, where the worth of every individual is upheld and strengthened, though what shame means in these religious groups will be different.

The power that shame exercises even in low-context communities and the need for congregations to become grace-full reminds me of *The Scarlet Letter* and the story of Hester Prynne. In seventeenth-century New England, Hester Prynne was accused of adultery. As a result, she had to wear a scarlet *A*, for adultery, on her clothing. She was publically shamed. Treated as more than guilty (having *made* a mistake), she was shamed because she *was* a mistake. The guilt of her lover, Arthur Dimmesdale, only became public when he revealed it himself, uncovering a similar *A*, which in his case was seared into the flesh of his chest. He lived with private guilt, she with public shame. This example also brings us to the awareness that gender may also play a role in how shame is allocated in society.

Like the feelings that I discuss in more depth, guilt and shame are related to connection, gender, power, and community. It is particularly important to examine these relationships in congregations that feel a sense of shame, or of being shamed, because of sexual misconduct or other serious breaches of trust by clergy or lay leaders. This need exists, as I have said in earlier chapters, because the work of making good decisions, building deeper community, and welcoming others into it is not just about our thoughts and actions. Often our feelings (and here I would include the complex web of thoughts, feelings, and cultural influences that make up shame and guilt) are the obstacles to healing and growth. Intentionally reflecting on shame and guilt, not just on cognitive understandings of what took place, will facilitate the move to a more grace-full community and establishing new guidelines for appropriate behavior.

Because I believe the areas of shame and guilt move beyond the most basic stimulus-response emotions, however, I refer readers to many fine works that have been written on these subjects. I am convinced that when individuals and congregations learn to more readily identify the six primary feelings and express them directly, rather than using learned substitutions, it will be easier for them to tackle the complexities of shame and guilt.

Resources

Gaede, Beth Ann, ed. *When a Congregation Is Betrayed: Responding to Clergy Misconduct.* Herndon, VA: Alban Institute, 2005. A comprehensive collection of essays dealing with a range of trust-shattering behaviors by clergy and how congregational leaders can respond to them to bring about congregational healing.

Herman, Judith Lewis. *Trauma and Recovery: The Aftermath of Violence—from Domestic Abuse to Political Terror.* New York: Basic Books, 1992. Herman is associate clinical professor of psychiatry at the Harvard Medical School and director of training at the Victims of Violence Program at Cambridge Hospital. She uses relational-cultural theory and her clients' own words to link domestic violence and social trauma.

Hopkins, Nancy Myers, and Mark Laaser. *Restoring the Soul of a Church: Healing Congregations Wounded by Clergy Sexual Miscon-duct.* Collegeville, MN: Liturgical Press, 1995. Commissioned by the Interfaith Sexual Trauma Institute, this pastoral book focuses on the healing of congregations following clergy sexual mis-conduct. It discusses the original problem of sexual misconduct and exploitation as well as neglected secondary victims of abuse: the congregation, the wider community, other clergy, the wider church, the offender's family, and the pastor who takes over.

Schmitz, Eileen. *Staying in Bounds: Straight Talk on Boundaries for Effective Ministry*. St. Louis: Chalice Press, 2010. This book develops the concept of boundaries from psychological and theological perspectives and discusses the benefits of boundaries. The author provides guidance for identifying, implementing, and enforcing healthy boundaries, with a special focus on ministry settings.

Chapter 10

Affectively Competent Congregations

What would a congregation look like if members took feelings seriously in all they did, and perhaps even consciously allowed their affective competence to shape their identity?

One given regarding healthy congregations is that they have a clear identity. Some congregations are known for their music program or for the quality of education and formation for children. Others are known for their outreach into the wider community and the ways that they engage in social justice ministry. Still others identify as intentionally multicultural congregations, places of radical welcome,[1] or "Open and Affirming" congregations.[2] A congregation I recently worked with has begun to see its purpose or mission as being a "safe place to have honest conversations about difficult issues." Any one of these missional statements or identities could give a community of faith a clear focus and serve as a rallying point for its members. Such a missional statement can also set the congregation apart from the other faith communities in the town or city and attract new members. In the overall ecology of religious life, a diversity of congregational identities and purposes is good. This diversity parallels the biodiversity of the natural order, which promotes healthy ecosystems and reduces the risk of mass extinctions of species.[3]

Missional Ecclesiology

Missional ecclesiology is a way of understanding what it means to be the church. The heart of this recent movement that crosses denominations is based on the Latin term *missio Dei*, "the mission of God." Instead of thinking of the church's mission in the world, which often focuses on converting people in foreign countries to the Christian faith or doing social justice in the world, missional ecclesiology is about living into all that God intends here and now for us in our congregation and in the wider community of which we are a part. It is more about being than doing. The central *discernment* question for such an understanding of what it means to be church becomes, "What is God doing in the world?" That question is accompanied by the *wisdom* question, "What does God *want* to do?" People who talk about the missional church or missional leadership focus not so much on what the church *does*, but on what God is doing and who the church *is*.[4] When I use the term *missional identity*, then, I am talking about who a congregation understands itself to be as it reflects on what God is doing and wants to do here and now in this congregation. A missional statement is that congregation's declaration to others about who it sees itself to be. When I combine the term *missional* with affective competence and suggest that a congregation could see its identity as forming a community grounded in and sharing affective competence with the wider world, what I am suggesting is that part of what God *does* here and now is give us feelings, and what God *wants* us to do is use those feelings to build deeper relationships, make better decisions, and help others also grow in affective competence. Developing a particular missional identity for a congregation does not mean inventing something totally new. Nor does it mean branding a congregation to sell it to others. It is more like seeing the statue within the block of marble and freeing it by chipping away the marble.[5] In theological language, finding the missional identity of a congregation means believing that God has given particular gifts to a community of faith, and that it can discover those gifts and focus on them for its own well-being and as a way to witness to God's mission in the world. Just as the raw block of marble may contain many possible statues but the sculptor brings forth *one* statue, so any given congregation has many possible identities. It is the congregation's responsibility to discern what it believes God is leading it to see and to bring forth that way of being, of living, in its particular time and place.

Imagine a congregation that understood its missional identity to be an affectively competent group of people in order to more vibrantly reflect all that the Creator intended humanity to be. Such a congregation would work to train its leaders and to encourage all its members to learn about their own feelings and to be responsive to the messages their feelings carried. The central organizing principle of this congregation—the way it identified itself and the image it held out to the wider community—would include serving as a resource for others who wished to become more affectively competent. Such a congregation would be a great gift to the community in which it was located. Individuals and groups stuck in patterns of poor communication might turn to such a congregation to get support and coaching in order to break through those patterns by seeing how their feelings blocked them from hearing one another. And because the messages that feelings carry are often opportunities to deepen relationships, faith communities could deepen the bonds among members and open new opportunities for relationships with people beyond their membership.

For a congregation to discern that affective competence lies at the heart of its missional identity does not mean that it creates this understanding *ex nihilo*, out of nothing. Rather, God has given feelings, or the neurological and emotional software of affective interactions, to all human beings.[6] Discerning a missional identity based on affective competence would mean that a church feels called by God to develop that particular skill as the living embodiment of the Divine in its corner of the world. If a congregation chooses affective competence as its missional identity, it should embrace affective competence fully. In the same way that a great artist would not think to dip her toe into beauty, but rather would embrace beauty in its fullness, so a faith community should embrace its missional identity fully—expressing it in every aspect of its life and ministry.

Even if a faith community did not choose to make affective competence its organizing purpose or missional identity, a congregation benefits when its members become more skilled in recognizing their own feelings and the feelings of the other members. In such a community, communication is more direct and effective. Meetings run more smoothly. The causes and dimensions of conflict are more identifiable and thus more appropriately engaged. Whatever the missional identity (for instance, "being a place where it is safe to have hard conversations," or "expressing our faith through the gift of music"), people will be better equipped to live that identity if they are affectively competent. Members would have the added benefit of building deeper relationships with one another, because they would be attending to the affective dimensions of each person in the congregation. This would mean that in addition to noticing and reflecting on what people believed (cognitive) and what they did (behavioral), they would notice their differences and similarities in regard to their feelings (affective) about their diverse beliefs and their various commitments to action, whether educational, liturgical, pastoral caring, or social justice.[7]

I have written a companion to this book entitled *Congregational Resources for Facing Feelings*, which includes a number of applications that explore some of the implications that a focus on affective competence can have in various areas of the life and ministry of a faith community. These applications can be purchased as a collection or individually. The application areas I have chosen are not meant to be exhaustive but rather to suggest what attending to and reflecting upon feelings might mean to various individuals and groups within a congregation. It is my deep belief that the work of developing affective competence should not be relegated to one corner of the faith community, such as the governing board or adult education. To do so would be analogous to focusing on the health of only one part of the body, for example the respiratory system, or going to the gym to develop one's left bicep.

I am suggesting a holistic or systemic intervention, a change that will touch every part of the community over time. Certainly each congregation will need to consider where it makes most sense to begin this work, or if it has begun, how to strengthen the affective competence in that area and then expand into the other sectors of the faith community. As with developing many other skills or competencies, the initial work seems difficult, because it means breaking old habits. Most people also feel self-conscious at the beginning, because developing affective competence involves slowing life down and being very intentional. It is a little like learning to ride a bike, learning to knit, or beginning to throw clay. One needs to take a step at a time. The process certainly doesn't look fluid for most beginners. And when we compare ourselves to those who are already proficient, we may feel inept and discouraged.

For those who have such fears, I would say that few new endeavors I have tried have had a more immediate and more profound payoff. I have also seen significant and direct results for participants in all the workshops and retreats I have led. That is not to say anyone comprehends the whole process right away. At the same time, nearly everyone who earnestly desires to improve his or her affective competence finds some very practical way in which a relationship takes a turn for the better. Congregations that embark on this work have more energy and focus. In short, the struggles bear fruit, fruit that will last, for the work that we are about is making greater use of the gifts that the Creator designed into our very being.[8] When we are becoming more affectively competent, we can be sure we are about God's work. We are participating in the *missio Dei*, the mission of God.

Conclusion

The affective software we were given at birth was designed by God to help us understand and interpret the world. Our feelings carry messages that help us know what we need and what choices are available to us. So feelings play a personal role in what we know and how we learn. Feelings are also highly relational. When our expression of feelings is congruent with the stimuli of a particular situation, that is when we are affectively transparent, other people are able to read what is happening to us emotionally, and they can choose how to respond to us with less ambiguity than if what we are expressing does not match what we are feeling.

Unfortunately, every one of us carries a certain amount of emotional baggage as we walk through the world. Nearly all of us have grown up in families that rewarded the expression of certain feelings and discouraged the expression of other feelings. In most cases, the prohibition of expressing one feeling in early childhood led to substituting the expression of another feeling, which likely led people around us to misunderstand what we were actually feeling (for example, sadness instead of anger). Having misperceived our feeling, others likely responded inappropriately—for instance, by offering comfort rather than negotiating boundaries or expectations. And even when the prohibition was minimal in our family of origin, teachers, neighbors, and faith leaders may have either consciously or unconsciously placed unequal value on the expression of different feelings, thereby supporting a parental prohibition. When this distortion happened, patterns of substitution were reinforced.

If reading this book has helped you to imagine and experience your emotional system as a natural and God-given state, if you have learned to befriend and value each of the primary feeling families without any negative judgments or substitution, and if you have been able to learn on a personal level the messages your feelings convey, then my intent for writing the book will have been fulfilled. In addition, I hope this new understanding has resulted in the opportunity to practice a more authentic way of expressing your feelings. The result may be that this new way of expressing your congruent emotions is strange or awkward for you. Other people may comment that they have never seen you angry before or that you always seemed so happy in the past and now there are times you seem really sad. It could be that you formerly experienced just as much anger and sadness as the people around you but you substituted peace or joy for what you were actually feeling. It is even possible that someone will say, "I like the old you better." Learning to become more affectively competent and affectively transparent is much easier when you have the support of allies who are involved in the same learning and transformation.

In addition, whether you read the book on your own or as part of a group, I hope you have begun to discuss with others how the clear expression of feelings builds community and helps groups make better decisions. I have no doubt that the individual journey to greater affective competence is worthwhile. At the same time, I deeply believe that our congregations, schools, town meetings, scout groups, and businesses will gain from becoming more affectively competent and transparent. On a group or congregational level, this competence will likely require training, workshops, or retreats. The journey will need to be intentional, and the educational efforts will need to be concerted. Congregational and group leaders will need to set the tone and the pace for learning. Their support is crucial, because their power and influence is distributed throughout the system. Leaders may appear to have the most to lose when congregations become more affectively competent and transparent, because they are comfortable operating primarily within the cognitive realm. They are also used to centralized authority, which may be reinforced by suppressed feelings. In fact, leaders may actually benefit most from the widespread affective learning and transformation that results, because relationships will be stronger and deeper within the community, and decisions will be more efficient and effective. In addition, leaders have often learned to suppress many of their own emotions in order to fit particular leadership stereotypes (rational, as opposed to "touchy-feely"; objective, as opposed to subjective; determined, as opposed to whimsical or "swayed by emotions"). As leaders learn to trust their own affective dimension of learning and decision making and begin to enable and trust other people's expression of feelings, they begin to realize the oppressive nature of these false stereotypes and the way their own humanity has been restricted—a form of internalized oppression. In addition, leaders who are committed to widespread affective competence and transparency benefit from greater community buy-in on decisions. Member engagement in daily community life and in significant transitions and transformations will be deeper when individuals have engaged their affect as well as their intellect. While members' resistance to change may at first be vocal and extensive, leaders will quickly learn to welcome expression of feelings that will help them know if their plans are on target or need modifications, and if they are proceeding too fast or too slow to maximize their outcomes. They will understand that processing feelings is as important as giving more cognitive explanations and negotiating assumptions and expectations.

Communities that engage in the work of becoming more affectively competent also will notice that they become more effective in overcoming gender disparity and other forms of oppression. Because the relational work of women is frequently disparaged and "disappeared," to use Joyce Fletcher's term, focusing on affect (which is key in relational work) will maximize the contributions of women and ensure their greater participation. The likelihood of enhanced participation will also be true for other groups who have been historically excluded from positions of power and decision making: people of color, children, the elderly, newcomers to congregations, and so forth. One tool of subjugation and oppression—the suppression of feelings—is mitigated when all the participants in a system become affectively competent and transparent.

In the final analysis, individuals and communities are most healthy, vibrant, and engaging when they have a balance of cognitive, affective, and behavioral competencies—that is, when they are thinking, feeling, and doing things intentionally, transparently, and effectively. The balance is important. The affective competence I hope to foster by this book is not meant to replace or subordinate intellectual competence or behavioral expertise. All our cognitive, affective, and behavioral capacities are God-given and meant for our own welfare and for the benefit of our human communities, as well as all living beings. My intention has been to bring the three areas of learning and expertise into greater balance and to suggest that congregations might be the ideal place to enhance emotional learning. Some examples of what that learning might look like are developed in the companion to this book, *Congregational Resources for Facing Feelings*, available electronically as a collection or as individual downloads. My dream is that congregations will become learning centers for affective competence. I can even imagine that if they became training centers within their communities for those who long to live enriched affective lives, they might have a vibrant and viable mission in the world at a time when many congregations question why they exist or what they have to contribute.

Appendix A

Feelings as Messengers Chart

Feeling	Stimulus	Message	Need or Response
Fear	Real or perceived danger	There is danger. I am threatened or in peril. I find new ideas and relationships scary.	I need to get safe. I need to arrange for protection, support, or reassurance for trying new behaviors or ways of being.
Anger	Real or perceived violation	There is a violation. My boundaries have been crossed. My expectations have been smashed.	I need to set limits, to reestablish boundaries, to renegotiate expectations.
Sadness	Real, perceived, or anticipated loss	There is a loss. I am experiencing or anticipating bereavement. I liked things the way they were.	I need comfort, space, or support to grieve, remember, and let go (as appropriate).
Peace	Deep awareness of connectedness	I am centered. I am connected to God and myself (and others).	I need to continue to be focused, centered, or connected.
Power or Agency	Accomplishment or anticipated success	I am competent. I am able.	I need to continue to foster my own competence and to empower others.
Joy	Inner gratitude, awe, wonder	I am excited, happy.	I need to continue to relish the joy and share it as appropriate.

Adapted with permission from a VISIONS-Inc. training tool (www.visions-inc.org). See also William Kondrath, God's Tapestry: Understanding and Celebrating Differences *(Alban Institute, 2008).*

Appendix B

Feelings as Messengers Exercise: Completed Sample

1. Write one of the six feelings (peaceful, powerful, joyful, scared, mad, sad) in each the blanks below. You may use a feeling more than once or not at all.

Family of Origin

A Feeling most allowed for you: *peaceful*
B Feeling least allowed for you: *mad*
S Substituted feeling: *sad*

Community I Am in Now

AN Feeling most allowed: *joyful*
BN Feeling least allowed: *powerful*
SN Substituted feeling: *sad*

2. When you look at your feeling patterns, what do you notice?
   I have a pattern of substituting sad *for other emotions I am not allowed to express.*

3. What similarities or differences do you notice in your early pattern and your pattern now?
   As a child, I couldn't express mad. *In my current community I have trouble expressing* powerful. *In both cases I substitute* sad. *I notice* scared *does not show up early or now.*

4. Place the letters **A, B, S** and **AN, BN, SN** on the chart below, next to the feelings you have identified above. Draw an
arrow from **B → S** and from **BN → SN.** These show your
substitution patterns.

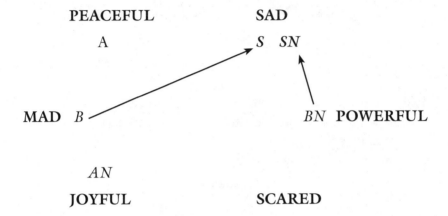

Appendix C

Outline of Feelings Retreat or Workshop

Note: The purpose of this outline is to demonstrate that it is possible to give a board or other group meaningful training in affective competence in a relatively short amount of time (four hours). Most congregations would need an outside consultant or trainer who is familiar with the material to lead the process, though as congregational leaders become more experienced and adept in their own affective competence, they might adapt this outline to meet their needs. This book contains most of the content necessary to lead the retreat or workshop. Additional helpful material is found in my book *God's Tapestry*, as indicated in the outline.

Should you use this outline for a training workshop or retreat, please give appropriate copyright credit. I would also welcome receiving any revisions, additions, or suggestions, which can be send through my website: www.billkondrath.com.

Possible Objectives

- To reflect on *who* we are and *how* we work together as leaders.
- To understand our differences and similarities in order to work together better.
- To come to know better the people with whom we share the ministry of leadership.
- To deepen our affective competence as leaders.
- To explore the relationships of differences, change, conflict, and commitment to community.

Agenda

9:00   Arrive (coffee and food available)

9:15   Opening worship
       Offer an opening prayer.
       Then in groups of six or seven, using the so-called African
       Bible Study method, discuss Matthew 14:22–33. In each
       group, the passage is read by three different people. Fol-
       lowing each reading, the group focuses on one question
       in this order:

1.   What word or phrase jumped out for you? (Each
     person responds with a word or phrase. No explana-
     tions. No cross-talk.)
2.   What do you think was going on in this story? (Each
     person has a chance to respond.)
3.   What do you think this story has to say to as we
     gather today? (Each person has a chance to re-
     spond.)

9:40   Overview of the day

9:45   Guidelines for our work together—presentation
       (25 minutes) and exercise

       Guidelines

       "Try on." (Be willing to entertain new thoughts, atti-
           tudes, beliefs, and feelings.)
       It's okay to disagree; it's not okay to blame, shame, or
           attack—self or others.
       Practice self-focus ("I" statements, notice your own
           feelings).
       Practice "both-and" thinking.
       Notice both process and content.
       Be aware of intent and impact.
       Practice confidentiality.
       Exercise (in pairs).

Which guideline seems natural to you, or which one are
you good at?

Which guideline is challenging for you, especially across
differences in gender, age, race, belief, or another
difference?

Processing Exercise (as a whole group)

What did you learn about yourself?

How might these guidelines be helpful to us in our
congregation?[1]

10:20 Break

10:35 Presentation on Feelings as Messengers

Three dimensions of learning and change (5 minutes,
chapter 1)

Presentation of six feeling families and substitution of
feelings (chapters 2–8)

11:00 Group Exercise

Part 1: My Feelings in My Family of Origin

(20 minutes)

1. Which of the six feelings was most allowed for you
   in your family of origin?
2. Which of the six feelings was least allowed for you in
   your family of origin?
3. What feeling did you substitute for the feeling that
   was least allowed?

Complete directions for this exercise can be found in *God's
Tapestry*, 98–99. In brief, ask participants to gather in the
center of the room. Tape six large sheets of paper, each
with one of the feelings, on the walls around the room. Ask
participants to move in silence toward the feeling that best
answers each question. Invite a few people to say something about what growing up was like when X feeling was
allowed, not allowed, or became the substituted feeling.

Part 2: My Feelings in This Congregation (20 minutes)

1. Which of the six feelings are you most allowed to express in this congregation?
2. Which of the six feelings are you least allowed to express in this congregation?
3. What feeling do you substitute for the feeling that is least allowed?

As in the first part of the exercise, people move in silence to the feeling that answers the question. Invite some verbal responses before moving in response to the next question. With large groups, the written exercise in chapter 8, "Feelings as Messengers," can be substituted for the exercise in which people move. You may ask participants to share their responses in small groups.

11:45 Break
12:00 Implications for us as individuals and as a community
       In groups of six or seven, ask participants the following questions:

1. What did you learn about yourself during this exercise?
2. How is your substitution pattern in your family of origin the same as or different from any substitution pattern you may exercise now?
3. Since a substitution pattern causes others to misinterpret your emotions, you are not likely to get the response that you may want or need. How might you choose to act differently so that you have a higher likelihood of getting desirable responses?
4. How might substitution patterns hinder how we function as a community? Can you name any areas in which we might be particularly vulnerable to a particular substitution? For example, do we expect children to usually be joyful? Do we prohibit teens or clergy or women from expressing anger?
5. What further questions do you have about feelings or emotional competence? What further education or training would you like to see offered in the congregation?

12:40 Wrap-up
       In the whole group, allow time for groups or individuals
       to respond aloud to questions 4 and 5.
12:55 Closing prayer or hymn

Notes

Introduction

1. A popular website that attempts to deal with the distinction of gender identity, gender expression, biological sex, and sexual orientation (or to whom we are attracted) can be found at the It's Pronounced Metrosexual website, http://itspronouncedmetrosexual.com/2011/11/breaking-through-the-binary-gender-explained-using-continuums. The site is hosted by Samuel Killerman, a writer and performer who uses those skills to advance progress in the realms of LGBT equality and social justice. He portrays the distinctions through a simple illustration called the Genderbread Person. The content of the website is continually modified as people write in to critique the terminology. These critiques are as important as the visual images because the terminology is continually changing and being nuanced.

2. See the work of Antonio R. Damasio, who is the David Dornsife Professor of Neuroscience, Psychology, and Neurology and director of the Brain and Creativity Institute at the University of Southern California. His books include *Self Comes to Mind: Constructing the Conscious Brain* (New York: Pantheon Books, 2010); *The Feeling of What Happens: Body and Emotion in the Making of Consciousness* (New York: Harcourt, 1999); *Looking for Spinoza: Joy, Sorrow, and the Feeling Brain* (New York: Harcourt, 2003); and *Descartes' Error: Emotion, Reason, and the Human Brain* (New York: Grosset/Putnam,

1994). Also see Joseph Ledoux, who is a professor at the Center for Neural Science at New York University. His books include *Synaptic Self: How Our Brains Become Who We Are* (New York, Viking, 2002) and *The Emotional Brain: The Mysterious Underpinnings of Emotional Life* (New York: Simon and Schuster, 1998). Daniel Kahneman, *Thinking, Fast and Slow* (New York: Farrar, Straus & Giroux, 2011) is a very clearly written "tour of the mind," which describes the two systems by which we think. Kahneman is Senior Scholar at the Woodrow Wilson School of Public and International Affairs. He is also professor of psychology and public affairs emeritus at the Woodrow Wilson School, the Eugene Higgins Professor of Psychology Emeritus at Princeton University, and a fellow of the Center for Rationality at the Hebrew University in Jerusalem. He received the Nobel Memorial Prize in Economic Sciences (2002) for his work in psychology that challenged the rational model of judgment and decision making.

3. See the work of Amy Banks, a psychiatrist who specializes in post-traumatic stress disorder, relationships, and brain chemistry. She is an instructor in psychiatry at Harvard Medical School and Director of Advanced Training at the Jean Baker Miller Training Institute at Wellesley College. Her articles are available through Wellesley College, and she is currently researching and writing about neuroplasticity, the brain, and relationships. Also see Louis Cozolino, professor of psychology at Pepperdine University, *The Neuroscience of Human Relationships* (New York: W. W. Norton, 2006).

4. As an example of some of the physical changes associated with particular emotions, see Paul Ekman, Robert W. Levenson, and Wallace V. Friesen, "Autonomic Nervous System Activity Distinguishes among Emotions," *Science*, n.s., 221, no. 4616 (Sept. 16, 1983): 1208–10, http://www.jstor.org/stable/i298670. *Science* is currently published by American Association for the Advancement of Science.

Researchers and theorists name different primary feelings. The feelings in this study differ somewhat from those on which I focus. It is clear, however, that bodily changes are associated with particular feelings and one can learn to notice these. The following are some of the changes recorded in Ekman, Levenson, and Friesen's study.

Emotion	Specific Change in Heart Rate	Change in Skin Temperature
	(beats/min.)	(degrees C)
Anger	+8.0	+.16
Fear	+8.0	−.01
Distress	+6.5	+.01
Joy	+2.0	+.03
Surprise	+1.8	−.01
Disgust	−0.3	−.03

5. See Damasio, *Self Comes to Mind*, 101–25. Damasio also refers to an emotion as "a program of action, and the result of the action is a change of body state. . . . As an emotion unfolds, a specific set of changes occurs, and the feeling of the emotion maps are the result of registering a variation superimposed on the ongoing maps generated in the brain stem and in the insula" (120). An Aspen Institute interview entitled "Antonio Damasio: This Time with Feeling" is available at the FORA.tv website, http://fora.tv/2009/07/04/Antonio_Damasio_This_Time_With_Feeling#fullprogram.

Chapter 1: Three Dimensions of Learning and Change

1. By referring to this dominant culture, I am trying to point out a bias toward certain assumptions and norms compared to which other assumptions and behaviors are usually considered to be deviant or *less than*. For instance, in many studies, only men (and sometimes

primarily white men who are also assumed to be heterosexual) are the subject of research and the conclusions of
the research are applied to all people. (See the discussion
of Shelley Taylor's work on stress and gender in chapter
2 on fear.) The dominant paradigm is developed, maintained, and enforced by those with the most power in the
system or culture.

2. David Keirsey and Marilyn Bates, *Please Understand Me:
   Character and Temperament Types* (Carlsbad, CA: Pro-
   metheus Nemesis Book, 1984).

Chapter 2: Fear

1. Edmund Burke, *The Works of the Right Honourable
   Edmund Burke: A Vindication of Natural Society; An
   Essay on the Sublime and Beautiful, Political Miscellanies*
   (London: Henry J. Bohn, 1854), 88. Burke was an Irish
   political philosopher, Whig politician, and statesman who
   is often regarded as the father of modern conservatism.

2. *A Burst of Light: Essays by Audre Lorde* (Ann Arbor, MI:
   Firebrand Books, 1988), 53. This quotation is from the
   fifth section of the book and entitled "A Burst of Light:
   Living with Cancer." This section contains excerpts from
   journals Lorde wrote during her first three years of cancer. This entry was dated February 18, 1984 (Ohio).

3. Unpublished poem by James Carroll, author, playwright,
   Boston Globe columnist, known for his social commentary. Author of *Constantine's Sword; Jerusalem, Jerusalem; Crusade;* and *An American Requiem.* A copy of the
   poem was given to me by the author.

4. Joy Harjo, *How We Became Human: New and Selected
   Poems, 1975–2001* (New York: W. W. Norton, 2002),
   50–51.

5. For a full discussion of dysfunctional rescuing and other
   oppressive behaviors that are part of relationships where
   there is a historical imbalance of power, see William M.

Kondrath, "Understanding Power and Difference: Race as a Primary Example," in *God's Tapestry: Understanding and Celebrating Differences* (Herndon, VA: Alban Institute, 2008).

6. I do not believe that gender is binary. There is growing literature about the way individuals perform in gendered ways. That is to say, we are socially conditioned to behave in typical or stereotypical ways according to how our culture or social groups perceive men and women. See Judith Butler, *Gender Trouble: Feminism and the Subversion of Identity* (New York: Routledge, 1999).

7. See Samuel Shem and Janet Surrey, *We Have to Talk: Healing Dialogues between Women and Men* (New York: Basic Books, 1998). Samuel Shem is the pen name of Stephen Bergman. They have also written the screenplay *Bill W. and Dr. Bob* about the origins of Alcoholics Anonymous. The play has been performed in New York and several other cities and at regional and national AA conferences.

8. See Beth Azar, "A New Stress Paradigm for Women," *Monitor on Psychology* 31, no. 7 (July 2000): 46–47, available electronically at the American Psychological Association website, http://www.apa.org/monitor/julaug00/stress.aspx.

9. Shelley E. Taylor, *The Tending Instinct: How Nurturing Is Essential to Who We Are and How We Live* (New York: Henry Holt, 2002), 24. Leading up to this quote, Taylor refers to thirty scientific studies that look at what men and women do in response to stress—do they go it alone or turn to others for help? She writes, "Thirty studies show that women draw on their friends, neighbors, and relatives more than men do, whether the stress results from unemployment, cancer, fear of crime, a death in the family, or simple sadness. From a scientific standpoint, this is an amazing consistency. In the social sciences, you rarely see thirty studies all showing the same thing."

10. Vimala Thakar, *The Eloquence of Living: Meeting Life with Freshness, Fearlessness and Compassion* (San Rafael, CA: New World Library, 1989), 46. Thakar's own self-discovery led her to go beyond the inward journey and to become active in the Bhoodan Land Gift Program, which persuaded Indian landlords to give land to poor farmers. Through the 1950s, more than five million acres of farmland were redistributed.

11. Peter L. Steinke, *Congregational Leadership in Anxious Times: Being Calm and Courageous No Matter What* (Herndon, VA: Alban Institute, 2006); Edwin Friedman, *Generation to Generation: Family Process in Church and Synagogue* (New York: Guildford Press, 1985) and *A Failure of Nerve: Leadership in the Age of the Quick Fix* (New York: Seabury Books, 2007), published posthumously with editing by Margaret M. Treadwell and Edward W. Beal; Ronald Heifetz, Alexander Grashow, and Marty Linsky, *The Practice of Adaptive Leadership: Tools and Tactics for Changing Your Organization and the World* (Boston: Harvard Business Press, 2009).

Chapter 3: Anger

1. William Shakespeare, *Timon of Athens,* in *The Complete Works,* ed. Alfred Harbage (Baltimore, MD: Penguin Books, 1969), act 3, scene 5, line 57; Alcibiades to the senators.

2. Beverly Wildung Harrison, "The Power of Anger in the Work of Love: Christian Ethics for Women and Other Strangers," in *Making the Connections: Essays in Feminisst Social Ethics,* ed. Carol S. Robb (Boston: Beacon Press, 1985), 14–15. Harrison powerfully conveys the relational perspective of feelings in this article. She was professor of christian social ethics at Union Theological Seminary in New York and the first woman president of the North American Society of Christian Ethics.

3. William Drysdale, *Proverbs from Plymouth Pulpit: Selected from the Writings and Sayings of Henry Ward Beecher* (New York: D. Appleton, 1887), 25. Beecher was a theologically liberal American Congregationalist clergyman, reformer, and author.

4. *The Taming of the Shrew* (Harbage), act 4, scene 3, line 79; Katherine to Petruchio.

5. Aristotle, *Nicomachean Ethics*, in *A New Aristotle Reader*, 4th paperback ed., ed. J. L. Ackrill (Princeton, NJ: Princeton University Press, 1989), 386.

6. *Coriolanus* (Harbage), act 4, scene 2, line 50; Volumnia to Menenius.

7. Frederick Buechner, *Wishful Thinking: A Seeker's ABC* (San Francisco: HarperSanFrancisco, 1993), 2. Buechner (b. 1926) is a Presbyterian minister, theologian, and author of more than thirty books. I have also run across two frequently cited quotations that I could not confirm: "Anger is an acid that can do more harm to the vessel in which it is stored than to anything on which it is poured," attributed to Mark Twain, and "Holding on to anger is like grasping a hot coal with the intent of throwing it at someone else; you are the one who gets burned," attributed to Buddha. The prevalence of these two quotes in books and on the Internet speaks to the tendency to see anger only in a negative light.

8. Thomas Fuller, *The Holy State, and the Profane State* (London: Thomas Tegg, 1841), 160. Fuller lived from 1608 to 1661 and wrote this work in 1642.

9. Thinking of anger as a connective tissue parallels the invitation of some therapists for their clients to explore whether fighting is a form of intimacy.

10. Harrison, *Making the Connections*, 15. Also David W. Augsburger, *Conflict Mediation across Cultures* (Louisville, KY: Westminster John Knox Press, 1995), 113–42, for a discussion of cultural differences and the social construction of anger.

11. Beth Ann Gaede, ed., *When a Congregation Is Betrayed: Responding to Clergy Misconduct* (Herndon, VA: Alban Institute, 2006).

Chapter 4: Sadness

1. John Greenleaf Whittier, *Maud Muller* (Boston: Ticknor & Fields, 1869), 12.
2. Toni Stuart is a poetry writer, performer, and developer. Her work is based on the belief that the way we use words has the power to change our lives and the world around us. She is based in Cape Town, South Africa. Visit www.tonistuart.tumblr.com.
3. Malika Lueen Ndlovu, *Truth Is Both Spirit and Flesh* (Mowbray, South Africa: Lotsha Publications, 2008). Ndlovu is an internationally published South African poet, playwright, and performer. Through her brand New Moon Ventures, she is dedicated to creating indigenous collaborative works in line with her personal motto "healing through creativity." Visit her website www.malika.co.za for more information.
4. George Byron, *Complete Poetical Works of Byron* (Cambridge, MA: Riverside Press, 1905), 218. George Gordon Byron, sixth baron, commonly known simply as Byron, was a British poet and a leading figure in the Romantic movement.
5. Elisabeth Kübler-Ross, *On Death and Dying* (New York: Macmillan, 1969).
6. Melissa M. Kelley, *Grief: Contemporary Theory and the Practice of Ministry* (Minneapolis: Fortress Press, 2010).
7. Axel Schwaigert is a Metropolitan Community Churches pastor in Stuttgart, Germany, as well as a funeral home director. His story is an appendix of his DMin (2011) dissertation "Communal Grief in Relationship to HIV/AIDS" and can be accessed in the Episcopal Divinity School library, Cambridge, Massachusetts.

8. The *Diagnostic and Statistical Manual of Mental Disorders* is published by the American Psychiatric Association. DSM-IV is the fourth edition published in 1994 and updated in 2000.
9. Ira Byock, *The Four Things that Matter Most: A Book about Living* (New York: Free Press, 2004).
10. Much of this information comes from private conversations with former students Nancy Wilson (Moderator of the MCC), Axel Schwaigert, and Joshua Love.

Chapter 5: Peace

1. Vimala Thakar, *The Eloquence of Living: Meeting Life with Freshness, Fearlessness and Compassion* (San Rafael, CA: New World Library, 1989), 20.
2. Fiona Macleod, "Amadan," in *The Dominion of Dreams under the Dark Star* (New York: Duffield, 1910). Fiona Macleod was assumed for years to be a Celtic visionary and romantic of the late nineteenth century. The writer was actually William Sharp, who used the name to express "his inner female nature." The prayer-poem contained in the story "Amadan" was written in 1895 and echoes an early Scottish (Celtic/Gaelic) blessing. That blessing is probably best known in the version composed by John Rutter, "A Gaelic Blessing," a four-part choral arrangement with organ or guitar, commissioned in 1978 by the Chancel Choir of the First United Methodist Church, Omaha, Nebraska, in honor of minister of music, Mel Olson. A popular adaptation by Mary Rogers can be found in *Earth Prayers from Around the World: 365 Prayers, Poems, and Invocations for Honoring the Earth*, ed. Elizabeth Roberts and Elias Amidon (San Francisco: HarperSanFrancisco, 1991), 172–73.
3. Robert Browning, *Shorter Poems* (New York: Charles Scribner's Sons, 1909), 3.

4. Dylan Thomas, *The Poems of Dylan Thomas* (New York: New Directions, 1952), 225–26. Dylan Marlais Thomas (1914–53) is one of Wales's greatest poets. His other well-known poems include "Do Not Go Gentle into That Good Night" and "And Death Shall Have No Dominion."
5. Thakar, *Eloquence of Living*, 2.
6. Verve, 1964; Sony Music Entertainment, 1998, originally released by Sony Music Entertainment, 1963.
7. See Carol Gilligan, *In a Different Voice* (Cambridge, MA: Harvard University Press, 1982). In studies conducted by Gilligan, she found approximately an 80 percent correlation between men and what she referred to as the dominant voice (making decisions based on rights and responsibilities), and approximately an 80 percent correlation between women and the different voice (making decisions based on relationships). See also Judith Butler, *Gender Trouble: Feminism and the Subversion of Identity* (New York: Routledge Classics, 1990) for a discussion of gender as performance.
8. Psychiatrist Stephen J. Berman and psychologist Janet Surrey have worked with thousands of couples and write about three relational impasses between men and women: dread-yearning, product-process, and power over–power with. Their comments on the product-process impasse are instructive here. Samuel Shem and Janet Surrey, *We Have to Talk: Healing Dialogues between Women and Men* (New York: Basic Books, 1994). Samuel Shem is the pen name of Stephen Bergman.
9. Based on Carl Jung's psychology, the *judging* and *perceiving* dimensions of personality have to do with how a person deals with the outside world. *Judging* people prefer to get things done. *Perceiving* individuals prefer to stay open to new information and options.
10. Marilou Awaikta, *Selu: Seeking the Corn-Mother's Wisdom* (Golden, CO: Fulcrum, 1993), 92.

11. See Peter Senge, C. Otto Scharmer, Joseph Jaworski, and Betty Sue Flowers, *Presence: An Exploration of Profound Change in People, Organizations, and Society* (New York: Doubleday, 2004). *Presencing* is a term Scharmer coined that combines the concepts of presence and sensing.

12. C. Otto Scharmer, *Theory U: Leading from the Future as It Emerges—The Social Technology of Presencing* (San Francisco: Berrett-Koehler Publishers, 2009).

13. Senge et al., *Presence*, 113.

14. The Friends General Conference has a short article that includes guidelines for a clearness committee and additional reading and resources. See the FGC website, http://www.fgcquaker.org/ao/toolbox/guidelines-clearness-committees.

Chapter 6: Power (Agency)

1. Gil Bailie, *Violence Unveiled: Humanity at the Crossroads* (Crescent Ridge, NY: Crossroad, 1996), xv. Bailie attributes the quotation to a conversation he had with Thurman. Howard Thurman (1899–1981) was dean of Rankin Chapel at Howard University (1932–44), the first black chapel dean of a majority white university, Marsh Chapel at Boston University (1953–65), and a spiritual adviser to Martin Luther King Jr.

2. Sojourner Truth, *Ain't I a Woman? A Play Adaptation by Kirsten Childs* (Pelham, NY: Benchmark Education, 2007). This speech, delivered on May 29, 1851 at the Women's Convention in Akron, Ohio, was briefly reported in two contemporary newspapers, without a title and without the "Ain't I a woman" refrain, and a transcript was published in the *Anti-Slavery Bugle* on June 21, 1851. Twelve years later, during the Civil War, Frances Dana Barker Gage, who presided at the convention where the speech was delivered, published a different version of the speech, which carried the "Ain't I a woman"

refrain. The speech was also in a Southern black dialect, which Truth, a Northerner, would not have spoken. This version was published in *History of Woman Suffrage*, 2nd ed., vol. 1, edited by Elizabeth Cady Stanton, Susan B. Anthony, and Matilda Joslyn Gage (Rochester, NY: Charles Mann, 1889). It became the standard version. I have chosen that text, rendered without the Southern dialect.

Sojourner Truth's speech always reminds me of "I Am Woman," the song cowritten by singer-songwriters Helen Reddy and Ray Burton. Released in its most well-known version in 1970, the song became an enduring anthem for the women's liberation movement. The import of the speech is also summed up in words widely attributed to Alice Walker: "The most common way people give up their power is by thinking they don't have any." Alice Malsenior Walker (b. 1944) is an activist and writer. She won the National Book Award and a Pulitzer Prize for her book *The Color Purple*.

3. Howard Thurman, *The Mood of Christmas and Other Celebrations* (Richmond, IN: Friends United Press, 1973), 22. Reprinted by permission of the publisher.

4. George Bernard Shaw, *Back to Methuselah: A Metabiological Pentateuch* (New York: Oxford University Press, 1947), 5. Shaw was an Irish playwright and cofounder of the London School of Economics and Political Science. He is the only person to have been awarded a Pulitzer Prize for Literature (1925) and an Academy Award (for *Pygmalion*, 1935). *Back to Methuselah* was written in 1921. The spirit of this quote is also captured by the words attributed to Don Miguel Ángel Ruiz: "And you say that it looks impossible to become what we really are, to be authentic, to be ourselves again. But I will tell you that it is much more difficult to try to be what we are not." Ruiz (b. 1952), a Mexican author of New Age spiritualist and neoshamanistic texts, wrote *The Four Agreements* (1997).

5. Viktor E. Frankl, *Man's Search for Meaning* (1946; repr., New York: Mass Market Paperbacks, 1997), 86. Frankl was professor of neurology and psychiatry at the University of Vienna Medical School and Distinguished Professor of Logotherapy at the US International University. He founded what has come to be called the Third Viennese School of Psychotherapy (after Freud's psychoanalysis and Adler's individual psychology)—the school of logotherapy. During World War II he spent three years at Auschwitz, Dachau, and other concentration camps.

6. New York: Platt & Munk, 1954.

7. As I watched the USA women's gymnastics team in the London 2012 Olympics, I sensed their gold medal performance was in large part due to their feeling of power, their sense that they would perform their routines to the best of their ability. This feeling was not power over their competitors but a sense of their own agency. The silver medal team from Russia was certainly talented, but seemed not to have the sense of power that the USA team displayed.

8. Jean Baker Miller, *Toward a New Psychology of Women* (Boston: Beacon Press, 1976). Miller analyzes gender and power in society and squarely places relationships at the center of human development. Joyce F. Fletcher, *Disappearing Acts: Gender, Power, and Relational Practice at Work* (Cambridge, MA: MIT Press, 1999). Fletcher stresses the need organizations have for relational skills and emotional intelligences and how organizations prevent women who exercise these skills from advancing.

9. Jean Baker Miller, "What Do We Mean by Relationships?" Work in Progress no. 22 (Wellesley, MA: Stone Center, Wellesley College, 1986), 9. The emphasis is Miller's.

10. Fletcher, *Disappearing Acts*, 64. Fluid expertise requires the skills of empowering others and being able to be empowered, that is the ability to learn from and be influenced by others above you, beside you, and below you in

seniority and status. See chapter 5, "Relational Theory as a Way of Valuing Differences," in my book *God's Tapestry: Understanding and Celebrating Differences* (Herndon, VA: Alban Institute, 2008), for a more detailed discussion of team-building, mutual empowerment, and fluid expertise.

Chapter 7: Joy

1. Lord Byron, *The Complete Poetical Works*, vol. 5, *Don Juan*, ed. Jerome J. McGann (Oxford: Clarendon Press, 1980), 142.

2. *The Complete Sonnets, Songs and Poems of William Shakespeare*, ed. Henry W. Simon (New York: Pocket Books, 1951), 13. The final quote carries the meaning that "you will amount to nothing by remaining single." It may be an allusion to the common saying "one is no number." This echoes Byron's notion that joy is born a twin.

3. *The Poems of Gerard Manley Hopkins*, 4th ed., edited by Gardner and MacKenzie (Oxford: Oxford University Press, 1970). Used by permission of Oxford University Press on behalf of The British Province of the Society of Jesus, www.oup.com. Gerard Manley Hopkins, SJ (1844–93), was an English poet, Roman Catholic convert, and Jesuit priest whose posthumous fame established him among the leading Victorian poets.

4. Emily Dickinson, *The Poems of Emily Dickinson*, ed. R. W. Franklin (Cambridge, MA: The Belknap Press of Harvard University, 1999), poem 143, written ca. 1860. Born in Amherst, Massachusetts, Emily Dickinson (1830–86) is now considered one of the greatest American poets, and yet fewer than a dozen of her nearly eighteen hundred poems were published during her lifetime.

5. Vimala Thakar, The Eloquence of Living: Meeting Life with Freshness, Fearlessness, and Compassion (San Rafael, CA: New World Library, 1989), 17.

6. According to the Daisaku Ikeda Words of Wisdom Committee, this quotation is the authoritative translation
   from the January 23, 1990, issue of the Seikyo Shim-
   bun, the Soka Gakkai daily newspaper published at the
   youth conference of Shizuoka Prefecture, held at the
   Fujinomiya International Culture Center on January 21,
   1990. Permission was obtained for the publication of
   this quotation. Many of the authoritative translations can
   only be found on the Words of Wisdom website, http://
   www.ikedaquotes.org. Ikeda (b. 1928) is a Buddhist
   leader, peace builder, prolific writer, poet, educator, and
   founder of many cultural, educational, and peace research
   institutions around the world. He has developed and in-
   spired what may be the largest, most diverse international
   lay Buddhist association (Soka Gakkai International) in
   the world today. Based on the seven-hundred-year-old
   tradition of Nichiren Buddhism, the movement is char-
   acterized by its emphasis on individual empowerment
   and social engagement to advance peace, culture, and
   education. Nichiren Diashonin (*Diashonin* meaning
   "great sage") was a Buddhist monk who lived during the
   Kamakura period (1185–1333) in Japan, a time rife with
   social unrest and natural disasters. Nichiren taught devo-
   tion to the Lotus Sutra as the exclusive means to attain
   enlightenment and chanting Nam-Myōhō-Renge-Kyō as
   the essential practice of the teaching. The Lotus Sutra af-
   firms that all people, regardless of gender, capacity, or social standing, inherently possess the qualities of a Buddha
   and are therefore equally worthy of the utmost respect.
7. See my book *God's Tapestry: Understanding and Celebrating Differences* (Herndon, VA: Alban Institute,
   2008). The first chapter, "Guidelines for Recognizing
   and Valuing Differences," discusses guidelines for working across differences and the theological rationale for
   each.

8. Jean Baker Miller, "What Do We Mean by Relationships?" Work in Progress, no. 22 (Wellesley, MA: Wellesley College, 1986).

9. Daisaku Ikeda, *Life: An Enigma, a Precious Jewel,* trans. Charles S. Terry (New York: Kodansha International, 1982), 185.

Chapter 8: Substitution and Projection

1. *Macbeth* (Harbage), act 4, scene 3, lines 228–9; Malcolm to Macduff.

2. S. R. Dube, R. F. Anda, C. L. Whitfield, et al., "Long-term Consequences of Childhood Sexual Abuse by Gender of Victim," *American Journal of Preventive Medicine,* (2005) 28, 430–8. Sixteen percent of males in the study were sexually abused by age eighteen. See also www.1in6.org.

3. *Emotional literacy* is recognizing what feeling I am experiencing and its congruence with the stimulus that provoked it. I can be experiencing more than one feeling at a time. Emotional literacy also extends to accurately noticing the feelings of other people. *Affective competence* is applying what I am learning about my feelings and the feelings of others in service of deepening relationships and getting tasks accomplished. Affective competence, like cognitive competence, has an interactive, utilitarian component.

4. Dylan Thomas, "Do Not Go Gentle into That Good Night," *The Poems of Dylan Thomas,* rev. ed. (New York: New Directions, 2003), 239.

Chapter 9: Shame and Guilt

1. Karen A. McClintock, *Shame-Less Lives, Grace-Full Congregations* (Herndon, VA: Alban Institute, 2012), 20. McClintock is also author of *Preventing Sexual Abuse in Congregations: A Resource for Leaders* (Herndon, VA:

Alban Institute, 2004) and *Sexual Shame: An Urgent Call to Healing* (Minneapolis: Fortress Press, 2001), and coauthor with Kibbie Simmons Ruth of *Healthy Disclosure: Solving Communication Quandaries in Congregations* (Herndon, VA: Alban Institute, 2001).

2. Ibid., 22.
3. Ibid., 175.
4. William M. Kondrath, *God's Tapestry: Understanding and Celebrating Differences* (Herndon, VA: Alban Institute, 2008), 4–5. The other guidelines include the following: try on process and content; practice self-focus; practice "both-and" thinking; be aware of intent and impact; take 100 percent responsibility for one's own learning; maintain confidentiality; it's okay to be messy; and say ouch.
5. Oppression has to do with how power is exercised by historically included or dominant groups; that is, those groups that have historically had more access to goods, resources, positions of power, and privilege as compared to groups that are historically excluded or targeted to receive fewer goods and services, and thus whose chances of survival or thriving are reduced. For this reason, I have chosen historically excluded or targeted groups when speaking about who is shamed because of their difference. An individual from a dominant or historically included group might experience personal-level prejudice. For example, a group of Latinos may exclude a white man from their group, but this is less likely to be experienced as shame by the white man. He is less likely to see it as an attack on his very being, in part because his white privilege genuinely offers him significant advantages relative to all people who are not white, if economic status, education, and so forth are relatively the same. For an in-depth discussion of the complexities of racism and other forms of oppression, see *God's Tapestry*, chapter 2, "Understanding Power and Difference: Race as a Primary Example." The point here is to notice that while it is possible for any individual to shame someone

else (or himself or herself) or to be shamed by any other individual, the impact of shame is different because of the way oppression treats people as less than based on their group membership.

6. Strokes can be given, received, rejected, and asked for, as well as given to oneself.

7. To be most helpful, feedback should be descriptive (not evaluative), specific (not general), appropriate to the needs of the receiver, useable, requested when possible (rather than imposed), timely, clear (checked with the receiver), and accurate (checked for reality; not simply one person's opinion).

8. Edward T. Hall, *Beyond Culture* (New York: Anchor Books/Doubleday, 1976).

9. Though the United States is mostly a low-context culture because historically it has been dominated by white European-descended peoples, it is important to notice the way in which our diverse cultural origins influence the attitudes, behaviors, and feelings of nonwhite groups within the United States.

Chapter 10: Affectively Competent Congregations

1. See Stephanie Spellers' engaging book *Radical Welcome: Embracing God, the Other, and the Spirit of Transformation* (New York: Church Publishing, 2006) for practical ideas about how to become more conscious and deliberate in the hard work of welcoming and embracing people who are not represented in your congregation.

2. Open and Affirming (ONA) is the United Church of Christ's designation for congregations, campus ministries, and other bodies in the UCC that make a public covenant of welcome into their full life and ministry to people of all sexual orientations, gender identities, and gender expressions. The designation was adopted at its General Synod in 1985, when they called upon

congregations to covenant as Open and Affirming. See the UCC web page Open and Affirming in the UCC, http://www.ucc.org/lgbt/ona.html.

3. The United Nations General Assembly declared 2011–2020 the United Nations Decade on Biodiversity (Resolution 65/161). See the United Nations Decade on Biodiversity website at http://www.cbd.int/2011-2020/.

4. Luther Seminary in St. Paul, Minnesota, has a Center for Missional Leadership and offers both a PhD and a DMin in congregational mission and leadership. They have also held an annual consultation on missional leadership for seven years. I have relied on the descriptions of Craig Van Gelder for my explanation of missional ecclesiology, including the central discernment and wisdom questions. See the Center's website, http://www.luthersem.edu/mission/default.aspx?m=3088, particularly the video *What Is Missional Church?* found on the website of the Center for Missional Leadership.

5. Michelangelo (1475–1564) is purported to have said, "In every block of marble I see a statue as plain as though it stood before me, shaped and perfect in attitude and action. I have only to hew away the rough walls that imprison the lovely apparition to reveal it to the other eyes as mine see it." See C. Edwards Lester, *The Artist, the Merchant, and the Statesman of the Age of the Medici and of Our Own Times* (New York: Paine & Burgess, 1845), 64, for a recounting of Michelangelo's inspirational process, which I am comparing to the practice of developing a missional identity.

6. I will leave for those more schooled in science to elucidate the question of sociopaths or others with severe emotional dysfunctions. The point I am making is that affective functioning is as universal to humankind as is cognitive or behavioral functioning, and as important—though it is often less valued for reasons I have described elsewhere.

7. I do not mean to imply that belief is simply a cognitive matter. In fact, I would argue that we bring our whole selves—thinking, acting, and feeling—to a relationship with God. At the same time, far too much of modern religious history has been focused on what individuals think or should think, and what they do or should do, to the exclusion of what they feel. I am inviting greater focus and attention on what individuals feel as an important dimension of their relationships with God, themselves, and others.

8. "You did not choose me but I chose you. And I appointed you to go and bear fruit, fruit that will last, so that the Father will give you whatever you ask him in my name" (John 15:16).

Appendix C: Outline of Feelings Retreat or Workshop

1. These guidelines are adapted from VISIONS, Inc., www. visions-inc.com. Further elaboration can be found in William Kondrath's *God's Tapestry: Understanding and Celebrating Our Differences* (Herndon, Va: Alban Institute, 2008), chapter 1.